The OFFICIAL
GUIDEBOOK *of*
Colonial Williamsburg

Containing a brief History of the City
and Descriptions of more than One
Hundred Dwelling-Houses, Shops, &
publick Buildings, *fully illustrated.*
Also a large Guide-Map.

MCM   LI

WILLIAMSBURG:
Printed for COLONIAL WILLIAMSBURG

ILLUSTRATIONS BY *Albert Koch*

Introduction

Each visitor to Williamsburg today steps back across the bridge of years to the little city which for nearly a century was capital of the Virginia Colony and focus of a proud plantation society. Eighteenth-century buildings, furnishings, and gardens again take their original form in this significant community. Trim carriages once more clatter along Duke of Gloucester Street, a broad public way described by the late President Roosevelt as "the most historic avenue in all America." Since 1927, when the first colonial house was acquired, the American past has been brought to life in an area nearly a mile in length. This work has been carried out by Colonial Williamsburg, Incorporated, a non-profit organization dedicated to the purpose "That the Future May Learn from the Past."

The visitor to Williamsburg will see the neat, weatherboarded houses of colonial days, with their broad brick Virginia chimneys, set in formal gardens, together with handsome English and American furnishings in the many buildings open to the public. Restoration work has been carried out to the smallest detail, whether in a modillion cornice, in the selection of authentic plants for each herb garden, or in accessories such as the "chagrine case of Raisors" in the governor's bedroom at the Palace. Every effort has been made not only to exhibit all this evidence of the past, but also to re-create a living community. The blacksmith works with ancient tools in shaping his metal, and the hostesses in the Exhibition Buildings wear appropriate farthingales.

These buildings and their landscaped gardens offer a laboratory in which the life and times of Washington, Jefferson, George Mason, Patrick Henry, George Wythe, Peyton Randolph, and other leaders may better be understood. Thus along with the texture and the fabric of the physical restoration should go understanding of the way of life of colonial Virginia and appreciation of the heritage created amid these impressive surroundings.

Williamsburg Becomes the Capital

The site of Williamsburg was first occupied in 1633 by Middle Plantation, a stockaded settlement erected against Indian attack by hard-pressed colonists from near-by Jamestown. As late as 1690, this outpost consisted only of a few houses, a mill, a smithy, and a store clustered around a small brick church and graveyard. Although the College of William and Mary was founded here in 1693—the oldest college, after Harvard, in the English colonies—Middle Plantation was little more than a village.

In 1698, however, the Statehouse at Jamestown was leveled by fire, and the legislators decided to move their capital to Middle Plantation, which they renamed Williamsburg in honor of the reigning English king, William III. Jamestown at that time was a crowded, cluttered town surrounded by brackish swamps which bred disease. It is easy to see why Williamsburg, serenely located on a broad ridge between the York and James rivers, was preferred.

From 1699 until the dark war year of 1780, when the capital was moved to Richmond, Williamsburg was the political, social, and cultural center of the entire colony. Here the royal governor lived, the Assembly convened, and the courts sat. Twice each year, when the legislature and courts were in session, crowds came to Williamsburg for "Publick Times." The population of the town (normally only about 1500) doubled almost overnight. Taverns were jammed. Shops were stocked with the latest goods imported from London. There were horse races, fairs, and formal balls. Auctions were held at various taverns and at Market Square. For six or eight weeks the city hummed with activity.

In Williamsburg's new H-shaped brick Capitol—the first statehouse to be called a "capitol" since the days of Greece and Rome—laws were passed affecting a vast territory which stretched westward to the Mississippi. Virginia was the largest and most populous of all the British colonies. Although distant settlements could never be fully controlled, every person in the enormous British domain of Virginia was subject to the government at Williamsburg—large planters and small freeholders in the Tidewater and Piedmont; merchants and dock hands at the busy wharves in Norfolk; settlers searching for pitch, tar, and turpentine in the Dismal Swamp on the North Carolina border; German emigrant ironworkers in Spotsylvania; tenants on Lord Fairfax's baronial estate of five million acres of the Northern Neck; frontiersmen and the agents of land speculators deep in Indian territory on the banks of the Ohio.

Williamsburg, however, was chiefly a planters' capital. Its ruling class was dependent upon the growth and sale of tobacco, that broad-leafed "Imperial weed" which John Rolfe had learned to cure in 1612. Some of the planters lived in the Piedmont, rolling country beyond the fall line of the rivers, but most of the leaders of this aristocracy came from the Tidewater. Presiding over a plantation which was a miniature village, the large planter lived most of the time in his mansion house, usually close by one of the many convenient waterways. But he spent many weeks of the year in Williamsburg, where he sometimes built or rented a town house for convenience when called to the city by politics or business. Otherwise he stayed in one of the numerous taverns, many of which were located along Duke of Gloucester Street near the Capitol.

The brief "house histories" which constitute the main text of this guidebook may offer some insight into the life of this bygone century. It was a crude society by modern standards. The death rate of children was appalling. The "average" man—perhaps the small freeholder—had little formal education. Wives had few legal rights. Boys were apprenticed to a trade when only fourteen. The brutal slave trade flourished. Besides the slaves, there were many white "indentured servants" (those who sold their services for a period of years in exchange for passage from Europe), living in a state of virtual bondage. Some of these were criminals whose sentences had been commuted to deportation.

Yet life in colonial Virginia had many rewards. The advancing frontier offered opportunities. Even those who were indentured could look forward to freedom and a future brighter than could usually be attained in England. It was also a hospitable period. There were country jigs as well as minuets; there was plenty to eat and drink; and the hand of authority did not bear too heavily on most Virginians. It was an age of change, activity, and promise.

Williamsburg and Revolution

Restored Williamsburg has a dual heritage. It recalls not only those years when Williamsburg served as the seat of government for Britain's largest colony in America, but also the turbulent period when it was the political headquarters for Virginia patriots who were to overthrow the rule of the Crown. It is an irony of history that the capital of Britain's "Old Dominion" is best known to posterity as a center of protest against British authority.

In the crucial decades before the Revolution, Williamsburg was a training and proving ground for leaders. Here George Washington, Thomas Jefferson, Patrick Henry, and Richard Henry Lee met and debated with other gifted contemporaries; their discussions and their written words did much to shape the course of America. When Williamsburg's own liberty bell in the trim belfry of Bruton Parish Church rang out the news of the Declaration of Independence, a significant period of transition came to an end; a transformation was complete. The city was changed from the proud capital of a crown colony to the even prouder capital of a new commonwealth in a new nation.

But, of wider importance than the concerns of one state or one country, eighteenth-century Williamsburg embodied concepts of lasting importance to all men everywhere:

The concept of the integrity of the individual. During the eighteenth century, man's respect for his fellow man grew. Politicians and philosophers alike shared a new awareness of the inherent dignity of every person. In colonial Virginia, this concept was best represented and expressed by Thomas Jefferson, although within the terms and conspicuous limitations of his time. As documents and debates of the period indicate, this appreciation of the importance of the individual was continuous and fundamental in the struggle for freedom and self-government. It remains today the essential motive of any free society.

The concept of responsible leadership. Virginia's planter aristocracy, trained to leadership from youth, accepted its public obligations without question. The ruling class, composed of the larger plantation owners, merchants, and professional men, felt a deep responsibility for the welfare of the colony. They willingly served as legislators in Williamsburg, as justices of the peace, and as vestrymen in their own parishes. Washington, for example, was conscientious both in attending sessions of the House of Burgesses and meetings of the vestry of Truro Parish. Such services were rendered whether or not they proved costly to private business ventures or inconvenient to personal plans. These characteristic qualities of experience and leadership in public affairs were of immeasurable importance in developing the generation of Virginia patriots who took an important part in the Revolution and in the formation of the new republic.

Belief in self-government. From 1619, when the first representative assembly in America met at Jamestown, Virginians increasingly came to believe themselves capable of handling their own public affairs. They recognized the traditional over-all authority and prerogative of the Crown, but resented any interference in their internal government on the part of a distant Parliament. Thus Patrick Henry dared to speak heatedly against the Stamp Act at the Williamsburg Capitol in 1765. Ultimately, when legal and constitutional means had failed to secure enough political autonomy for Virginians, the colonial leaders saw revolution and independence as the only means to achieve their ends. This devotion to the principles of self-government was the chief cause of the Revolution in Virginia.

The concept of individual liberties. Virginians believed that they, as British subjects, possessed important individual liberties and rights rooted in Magna Carta. The protection of these rights by colonial legislation culminated in the Virginia Bill of Rights. This classic document, drafted by George Mason and adopted unanimously in 1776 by the legislators assembled at the Capitol, asserted that "all men are by nature equally free and independent," and set forth in sixteen articles such fundamental rights as freedom of religion and the press; trial by jury; free elections; and the subordination of military to civil authority. Virginia's Bill of Rights influenced the Declaration of Independence and later became the basis for the first ten amendments to the Constitution of the United States. It is the greatest single document associated with Williamsburg, and has been influential in all free nations of the world.

The concept of opportunity. The colonization of Virginia is a chapter in the story of mankind's old dream of establishing a more abundant life in a new land. Those who undertook the hazardous and costly voyage did so chiefly because they wanted a better chance for themselves and their children. Virginia offered a new measure of individual and political freedom; a class structure less rigid than that of England; the economic opportunities of a growing colony; and the lure of new lands and a frontier pushing westward.

These five concepts were fused and given deeper significance by an underlying appreciation of the moral and spiritual values of life. The great Virginians of eighteenth-century Williamsburg faced personal or public problems with an abiding faith in God and their fellow men. This faith was basic to their life and work.

Today, Williamsburg stands as a symbol of one of the most impressive eras of the American past: an era of ideas as well as actions which together helped to shape a young republic. There is much in Williamsburg to recall the color and drama of the colonial city, and the eventful everyday life of Virginia's capital. There is also the opportunity to see Williamsburg as an affirmation of the spiritual vigor which must underlie any strong democratic society.

The Years Between

Williamsburg was the wartime capital of the young republic from 1775 to 1779. Later, during the last decisive campaign of the war, it served as headquarters first for Cornwallis and, after he had established his army at Yorktown, for Washington and Rochambeau. Though never a battlefield, the city did not escape the impact of war. Many of its men were killed and the wounded, carried on wagons over the twelve miles of muddy road from the battlefield, filled improvised hospitals at the Palace and Wren Building.

After 1780, when the capital was moved to Richmond, Williamsburg stepped backstage in history, to resume its role only when restoration work was begun in 1927. In the years between, however, the city occasionally saw exciting days as when, in 1824, Lafayette returned to be feted by the community. During the Civil War Williamsburg's strategic position on the Peninsula placed it between contending armies and it became briefly the headquarters of Union General McClellan and Confederate General Joseph Johnston. The Magazine was once again called into use for storing powder. But through most of these years Williamsburg was a small college town and county seat, its former importance buried in history and memory, as well as in the weathered colonial buildings which survived.

Town Plan of Williamsburg

Francis Nicholson, governor from 1698 until 1705, was justifiably proud of the town plan he devised for the new capital. A wide, 99-foot central avenue, named for the heir presumptive, the Duke of Gloucester, was terminated at one end by the Capitol and at the other by the College of William and Mary. The Governor allowed himself to be twice remembered in Francis and Nicholson streets which run parallel to Duke of Gloucester Street on either side. Market Square, a spacious public green, stands at the mid-point of the plan. At a right angle to the main axis—Duke of Gloucester Street—is a catalpa-bordered approach to the Palace. The plan of Williamsburg proved highly successful. Governor Nicholson envisioned a "green country town," with every house allotted a half acre of land. An ordinance, to insure uniformity, required the building of each dwelling "within six Foot of the Street." These were advanced principles of site planning. The orderly new capital of Virginia, growing rapidly, soon stood in marked contrast to Jamestown with its cramped and medieval row housing.

Architecture of Williamsburg

Colonial fashions in architecture, as in dress, were imported from England and the Continent, but, in the words of a contemporary, were "adapted to the Nature of the Country by the Gentlemen there." The architectural vogue of the Mother Country was naturally more evident in public buildings and in costly private mansions than in more common dwellings, and yet even the most pretentious structures of eighteenth-century Virginia were substantially modified because of local uses and needs, the climate, the building materials available in the region, and the scarcity of skilled labor.

Many public buildings and a few private dwellings and shops were made of brick, baked at local kilns and laid in the prevailing patterns of Flemish or English bond. Most early Williamsburg houses, however, were fashioned of wood, which was far less costly and (most people thought) less susceptible to dampness. These frame houses were most often painted white on the outside, although other colors were also favored. In spite of the fire hazards of an era of candles and the open hearth, many wooden buildings have survived, remaining sufficiently well preserved to permit their restoration.

Frame dwellings in Williamsburg have, characteristically, a steep-pitched A-roof, a gambrel roof, or a hipped roof. Gambrel-roofed houses often have a ground plan which is nearly square, whereas A-roofed houses usually have a rectangular ground plan, most commonly 20 by 40 feet. These houses are one or two rooms deep, with either a central or side hall. A broad-based brick chimney is almost always found at one end, and frequently at both. Outside shutters for frame houses and inside shutters for brick houses became increasingly common, offering privacy as well as protection from the midsummer sun. Interiors were often painted in bright colors and were enriched by mantels, molded cornices, chair rails, and frequently by paneling. Walls were rarely papered until late in the eighteenth century.

As protection against the odors and heat of cooking during summer weather, the kitchen was usually situated in a separate building at some distance from the house. Other outbuildings, customarily placed between the house and garden, included the smokehouse, well, and dairy, with the privy, more obliquely known as the "necessary house," further removed. There were usually, in addition, a stable and coach house.

Public Buildings

Most of the public buildings were erected during the time when Williamsburg was the capital of Virginia. The Wren Building antedates this period however; through many vicissitudes it has stood since 1695 at the center of the college yard and of college life. Other major buildings which at the time of restoration had maintained their function continuously since colonial times were Bruton Parish Church, the Courthouse, the Public Gaol, and, at the College, the President's House and the Brafferton. Though variously employed, the buildings of the Magazine and the Public Records Office, too, withstood the challenge of time. Of the public buildings, only the Capitol and the Palace had to be completely reconstructed.

These buildings resist definite classification in a single style. English and Dutch influences are conspicuous. Interest in the English Renaissance can be seen in the detail of graceful wood towers, modillion cornices, and arched windows, and in the symmetrical arrangement of interiors. This was, however, an architecture modified and modeled by local abilities, interests, and tastes. It was produced by talented master builders and local craftsmen, joiners, and bricklayers, who relied on experience and the simple architectural handbooks of the day rather than on formal drawings. Most buildings acquired a native expression, free from the ostentation which might have resulted from strict adherence to formal architectural orders.

Furnishings

The furnishings of the Exhibition Buildings are drawn from both England and America. Household goods in large quantity were shipped to Virginia from England in payment for tobacco, and the general character of American furnishings of the eighteenth century was determined by

English fashion. In the styles of Queen Anne's reign, much in evidence in Williamsburg, the cyma, or S curve, was an important departure, adding to the comfort as well as the grace of furniture. In the chairs, the curve of the cabriole leg was balanced by a curving back much kinder to the human frame than the stiff carved backs of the Jacobean period. In Queen Anne furniture, walnut replaced oak as the most favored wood.

During the eighteenth century, styles were for the first time identified with great cabinetmakers rather than reigning monarchs, and the style prevailing in America after about the middle of the century was known as Chippendale. The genius of Thomas Chippendale ushered in the age of mahogany—a wood well adapted to the rich carving and fine detail which, rather than any one form, characterized his work. Many of his pieces are to be seen in Williamsburg, with both the cabriole and straight leg. Chair backs range from an adaptation of the solid, curving, Queen Anne splat to elaborately pierced and "interlaced" splat backs.

A few examples have been included in the Exhibition Buildings of the work of Hepplewhite and Sheraton, expressing the lighter elegance introduced by the designs of the Adam brothers; this influence was not, however, extensively felt in America until after the colonial period.

Imported pieces were expensive to acquire and slow to arrive, and many of Williamsburg's furnishings were the work of local craftsmen. Cabinetmakers who boasted "a finer kind of joiner's work" were advertising in the *Virginia Gazette* by the middle of the century, and new impetus was given to their work when the colonists boycotted British imports. Benjamin Bucktrout, prosperous enough to occupy a fine house on Francis Street, was probably the city's best-known cabinetmaker.

Authorities who furnished the Exhibition Buildings were greatly assisted by inventories. When Governor Fauquier died in Virginia, a record of his possessions was kept, and

Governor Botetourt's executors prepared an itemized list-ing, room by room, including even minor accessories. Tavern keepers often took an inventory and some wills contained an appraisal of goods left by a householder to his heirs or creditors. Accounts kept at local auctions have been found and many letters and orders specifying items to be sent from the Mother Country. Documentary and archaeological evidence together made possible fidelity not only in furniture but in fabrics, glass, china, and even in such intimate details as the silver-rimmed spectacles beside an open book or the playing cards laid out on a table ready for a game. Where definite evidence was lacking, prece-dents of the period have been relied upon, together with a knowledge of those who lived in the buildings. The Palace, the Capitol, and the Gaol reflect in particular the reigns of William and Mary, Queen Anne, and George I, whereas the Wythe House and the Brush-Everard House, furnished by Virginians, contain many American-made pieces.

The search for furnishings has been conducted through-out the world and still continues. The handsome crystal chandelier in the Supper Room of the Palace, for example, was found in Canton, China. Reproductions are used rarely and are replaced as soon as originals can be located.

Gardens of Williamsburg

The gardens of Williamsburg, large or small, are general-ly formal, reflecting the orderly character of eighteenth-century architecture. Such mannered gardens must also have provided a pleasant contrast to the wilderness which surrounded the early colonists. A kitchen garden and plea-sure garden, with a few carefully selected fruit trees, were arranged in a balanced fashion and linked by marl or brick paths to the associated house, outbuildings, and service areas. Thus the typical Williamsburg layout was a minia-ture plantation compressed to fit a city lot.

Most gardens are based on English precedents, and offer strong evidence of the Dutch influence introduced into England by William and Mary. The designs, whether square, circular, oval, or rectangular, are usually outlined with fences, walls, or hedges of evergreen material such as box and holly; this extensive use of evergreens gives a distinctive character to Williamsburg gardens. Through most of the year color is added by flowers or by flowering trees and shrubs. Decorative walls, gates, and vases are used in the more elaborate gardens, and many include topiary work (trees or shrubs clipped to formal or quaint shapes).

In restoring Williamsburg gardens, landscape architects relied on excavations, manuscripts, old maps of the town and other southern colonial towns, and on studies of surviving colonial gardens in this general area. Only plants known to the colonists in the eighteenth century have been used.

The Restoration of Williamsburg

Two men are responsible for re-creating eighteenth-century Williamsburg, the Reverend W. A. R. Goodwin and John D. Rockefeller, Jr. The former, late Rector of Bruton Parish, long cherished a dream of preserving the historic past of the old city. He communicated this vision to Mr. Rockefeller who made funds available and assumed leadership and direction of the restoration work. The project, which is generally known as Colonial Williamsburg, consists of two corporations—Colonial Williamsburg, Incorporated, a non-profit educational corporation, and its wholly owned subsidiary, Williamsburg Restoration, Incorporated, which is concerned with business operations.

Mr. Rockefeller has provided funds in the amount of approximately $44,500,000 for this project. In recent years operating and maintenance costs have been met in the main by revenue from Williamsburg Inn and Lodge and their associated guesthouses and taverns; rentals; the Williamsburg Theatre; admissions to the Exhibition Buildings; and sales of authorized reproductions, gifts, and publications. Mr. John D. Rockefeller III is Chairman of the Board of Trustees of both Colonial Williamsburg, Incorporated, and Williamsburg Restoration, Incorporated. The two corporations employ more than one thousand persons.

The project was begun in 1927. The Raleigh Tavern was opened to the public in 1932, followed by the Capitol (1934), Governor's Palace (1934), Ludwell-Paradise House (1935), Public Gaol (1936), George Wythe House (1940), and Brush-Everard House (1951). The Magazine, exhibited for some years by the Association for the Preservation of Virginia Antiquities, was leased and reopened as an Exhibition Building of Colonial Williamsburg in 1949. Restoration work was completed at the Wren Building in 1931 and at Bruton Parish Church in 1940. Of all these buildings, only three (the Capitol, Palace, and Raleigh Tavern) had to be entirely rebuilt.

This guide will make constant use of two terms—*restored* and *reconstructed*. The former is applied to buildings which were still standing in whole form or in major part and needed only to be repaired and stripped of later additions. The latter is applied to structures which had fallen victim to fire or dismantling and had to be entirely rebuilt on their original sites. In all, eighty buildings have been restored, including a high percentage of those mentioned in house histories; approximately three hundred have been reconstructed, of which a very large number are outbuildings. In both types of work, architects have been guided by archaeological remnants, maps, drawings, and daguerreotypes; data from insurance records, diaries, and wills; and any other source of evidence which research workers could discover to shed light on the city's past. Where no definite evidence is available, reliance has been placed on architectural precedents and an examination of surviving colonial buildings in the Tidewater area.

To complete the "restored area" many additional buildings are planned; among them dwelling houses, taverns, and craft shops both for exhibition and private use. Some day perhaps both America's first theatre on Palace Green and the city's second theatre close by the Capitol will rise again on their eighteenth-century sites.

During restoration work, modern conveniences and services were hidden rather than discarded. Telephone and electric wires were buried and fire hydrants made inconspicuous. Houses to be used for residential purposes have modern plumbing, insulation, and other features which would have startled the colonial owners. Occupants of some of these houses are Williamsburg residents who allowed their homes to be restored and modernized—or demolished—in return for a lifetime lease of a colonial dwelling. Some obvious concessions have been made also for the convenience of the twentieth-century visitor: cobblestones and pavement replace mud and dust in the city's streets, and a few signs have been necessary. The business district on Duke of Gloucester Street, although designed in a manner to harmonize with colonial architecture, was developed to meet the modern requirements of businessmen. It should also be noted that the restored area, although conspicuous, constitutes only a portion of the City of Williamsburg.

Today there are about 6500 persons living within the city limits, although many residents of near-by counties use Williamsburg as a business or marketing center. There are no large industries. Two distinguished institutions founded in colonial days continue to take their place in the community—the College of William and Mary (1693), and Eastern State Hospital (1770). Williamsburg was chartered as a city on July 28, 1722. Its present government is administered by a mayor, council, and city manager.

A Note on the Guidebook

For the visitor's convenience in identifying buildings wherever he may find himself in Williamsburg, the house histories in this guidebook have been grouped by streets, with the street name given in a running head at the top of each page and the intersection of cross streets indicated where they occur. The streets are arranged in alphabetical order. The letter following a house name indicates on which side of the street the building is located. An index is also provided, and a map giving the names of houses and a key to buildings and gardens open to the public.

The restored area cannot easily be indicated with exactness. Its furthest limits are the Palace to the north, Waller Street to the east, and the College to the west. It includes, to the south, a large part of the property on Francis Street. Visitors will be able to distinguish the restored sections within these confines by the concentration of houses on the map. Because of their architectural, historical, or practical interest a few additional buildings which do not fall within the area—or the period—of restoration, have been included in the guide and on the map. Space has permitted the inclusion only of outbuildings conspicuously located.

The work of restoration, excavation, and reconstruction is still in progress and will continue for many years as further information becomes available. Changes which could be anticipated have been included in the house histories.

For help in planning an itinerary adapted to any desired length of time, visitors are urged to go first to the Reception Center on South England Street. A brief introductory program in motion pictures and color slides is presented there continuously during the day. Combination and single-admission tickets to the Exhibition Buildings are on sale. There is no charge for the program or advisory services. Bus service in the restored area is free to holders of combination tickets.

The Capitol

At the eastern end of Duke of Gloucester Street stands the reconstructed Capitol, one of the chief Exhibition Buildings of Colonial Williamsburg. For the better part of a century—from 1704 to 1780—Virginia's colonial government convened on this historic site. Here an embarrassed and stammering Washington was applauded by fellow burgesses for his part in the French and Indian War; here Patrick Henry defiantly protested the Stamp Act until accused of treason; here George Mason's Virginia Bill of Rights became law. At this place the House of Burgesses, America's oldest legislative assembly, held its meetings, together with the smaller, more aristocratic Governor's Council. The High Court of the Colony met in the paneled courtroom to sit in judgment on offenders of that bygone century.

The Capitol was ordered built by an act of 1699, less than one year after the last of several statehouses in Jamestown had succumbed to fire. As a drastic precaution against this danger, Williamsburg's first Capitol was designed without chimneys and the use of fire, candles, or tobacco was strictly prohibited. In time such safeguards were sacrificed to necessity and convenience; a secretary complained, for example, that his records were "exposed by the Damps." In 1723 two chimneys were added. Candles were brought in, and doubtless permission was soon granted to smoke tobacco—Virginia's "bewitching vegetable." Whether from these sources, or from arson (as was supposed at the time), the building was gutted by fire on January 30, 1747, "and the naked Brick Walls only left standing." With the encouragement of Governor William Gooch, the "Royal Fabric" was within a year ordered rebuilt, and a second capitol building was completed in 1753, incorporating the surviving walls of its predecessor but different in appearance. After the removal of Virginia's government to Richmond in 1780, the second building fell into disrepair and in 1832 it too was destroyed by fire.

Before reconstruction could be undertaken, Colonial Williamsburg faced a dilemma: should the first or second capitol building rise again on the old foundations? The second Capitol was of greater historic interest since it witnessed the events of the years before the Revolution, but the first Capitol could lay claim to greater architectural distinction. Long searching of the architectural evidence disclosed that voluminous files would permit the accurate reconstruction of the earlier building, whereas few records were available for the later. It is the first Capitol which is here reconstructed.

The foundations for the original building were laid in 1701. During its construction under the supervision of "master builder" Henry Cary, Virginia's lawmakers met in the Wren Building of the College but moved impatiently into the new Capitol in 1704, a year before its final completion was symbolized by the surrender of the builder's keys to the Speaker of the House of Burgesses.

The period of the Capitol is signified by the coat of arms of Queen Anne emblazoned on its tower, and by the Flag of the Great Union (the eighteenth-century form of the British Union Jack) which flies proudly overhead. The style of architecture, with round and arched windows, and a cupola, is of the Renaissance but simplification was imposed by conditions in a young colony, as evidenced by the absence of colonnades or an elaborate façade. The H-shaped plan is an early example of an architectural design successfully devised for a specific purpose. It also reflects the make-up of Virginia's colonial government. One wing is taken up by the Hall of the House of Burgesses (on the first floor) and committee rooms for the burgesses (on the second). The other wing, finished and furnished much more elaborately, houses the General Courtroom (on the first floor), and the Governor's Council Chamber (on the second). Each wing has its own staircase. On the second floor— appropriately linking the two wings—is the Conference Room, where burgesses and councilors met together for morning prayer, or held joint conferences to resolve disagreements. The composition of the building is set off by the tall hexagonal cupola and is skillfully defined on Capitol Square by a sturdy brick wall.

In Williamsburg's Capitol laws were enacted affecting the whole colony. The Governor, when he rode in his coach from the Palace to open the Assembly, was the symbol of the power of the Crown which extended from the sea to the huge wilderness empire then claimed by Virginia.

Legislators who met here included virtually every Virginian of note in the eighteenth century. The Capitol was the scene of constitutional opposition to what the colonists regarded as arbitrary policies of King and Parliament; here, claiming the rights and privileges of British subjects, Virginians sought to defend their concept of self-government—a concept which had taken root when the burgesses first met in Jamestown in 1619 and which had matured through the years. In the end the lawmakers reluctantly took up arms against the Mother Country; yet their prolonged effort to achieve their goal by peaceful means is a conspicuous testament to their respect for the processes of deliberation carried on within the walls of the Capitol.

The site and the original foundations of the Capitol were faithfully preserved over the years by the Association for the Preservation of Virginia Antiquities, and were generously deeded by that organization to Colonial Williamsburg for the reconstruction. The rebuilt Capitol was opened in 1934 by the House of Delegates and the Senate of the Commonwealth of Virginia, meeting in joint session. At this time a bill was passed enabling the General Assembly to convene in the colonial Capitol at times which might seem proper, a practice which in peacetime has been followed on some occasion during each session. At the dedication in 1934 the Assembly was addressed by Governor George C. Peery, and by John D. Rockefeller, Jr., whose discourse closed with the words: "What a temptation to sit in silence and let the past speak to us of those great patriots whose voices once resounded in these halls, and whose far-seeing wisdom, high courage and unselfish devotion to the common good will ever be an inspiration to noble living. To their memory the rebirth of this building is forever dedicated."

Public Records Office – N. Restored. After the Capitol was gutted by fire in 1747, the legislators decided to erect this separate building "for the Preservation of the Public Records and Papers." The sloping chimney caps designed to prevent downdrafts, the  plastered window jambs, and the stone floor all reflect the builders' fear of fire. The rubbed brick of the pedimented doorway is considered exceptionally fine. The rounded front steps, similar in design to others in Williamsburg, are of blue Shrewsbury stone. After the capital moved to Richmond, the building was used for court offices, and by 1855 had been transferred to private ownership. The frame wing at the rear of the building is modern. Privately occupied.

Kerr House – S. Restored. Alexander Kerr, a Scottish jeweler and merchant, built this brick house in 1736. During the Civil War, by which time it had been considerably enlarged, the house served as military headquarters first for Confederate General Joseph Johnston and then for Union General George McClellan. In colonial times the property, advantageously situated near the Capitol, accommodated other buildings: one, a store, was destroyed by fire in 1754 because the storekeeper, according to a neighbor's report, left a fire  "too carelessly" while he "staid longer than he had intended at a Public House." A snuff mill was later operated here by John Drewidz and Charles Hunt, and, after them, by the firm of Hunt and Adams. Privately occupied.

Burdette's Ordinary–N. Reconstructed. A swinging sign of Edinburgh Castle hangs where John Burdette once kept his ordinary. It was a typical, run-of-the-mill tavern, used chiefly for drinking and gambling. Meals were sometimes served, and during Public Times the rooms were pressed into service for group sleeping. At Burdette's death, his inventory included the characteristic effects of his trade: numerous "crackt" plates, "1 old Fiddle," "1 billiard table with sticks, balls, etc.," "11 pr. dice," and "a Quantity of choice old Madiera Wine, and old Barbados Rum." A sketch clearly showing

the unusual one-and-a-half story porch chamber was drawn in 1743, as evidence in a lawsuit concerning the property line between the Ordinary and the Red Lion next door. The survival of this document made accurate reconstruction possible. Privately occupied.

The Red Lion–N. Reconstructed. In 1717 the trustees of Williamsburg granted this lot to Francis Sharp. Sharp apparently complied promptly with a building clause, then customary, requiring that a building be erected within twenty-four months, for the following year he obtained a license to offer "good, wholesome

and cleanly lodging and diet for travellers." He agreed to forbid "any unlawful Gaming . . . nor on the sabbath day [to] suffer any person to tipple or drink more than is necessary." The early house is shown in the sketch mentioned in connection with Burdette's Ordinary next door. In the 1930's an elderly resident described the house as he remembered it after the Civil War. During the eighteenth century several additions had been made, expressed in the reconstruction by three entrances, for as many as three tenants are known to have occupied the house at one time. The name Red Lion has long been associated with this house, but new evidence proves that the original Red Lion was further west. Privately occupied.

Nicolson Shop–N. Restored. This distinctive red building is representative of the two-story frame shops which were common in

eighteenth-century Williamsburg. As in other examples, the second floor was used for residence or storage. The property was first owned by John Marot, a French Huguenot who was once secretary to William Byrd II; later Marot operated a tavern here. The tavern was eventually replaced by this shop, which Robert Nicolson acquired in 1773. Dismantling of a large nineteenth-century building exposed the original framework, now restored. Remnants of colonial wallpaper were also found in the course of alterations. Privately occupied.

Pasteur-Galt Apothecary Shop–N. Reconstructed. A mortar and pestle on the gaily painted sign identify this shop as that of an apothecary. Open to the public as a craft shop, it exhibits for today's visitors the imposing array of "elixirs" and "ointments" of colonial medicine and "compleat Setts of amputating Instruments." Delftware jars of medicinal herbs and aromatic spices line the proprietor's

shelves, and perfume, tobacco, and other wares are carried as valuable side lines just as they were in colonial days. The eighteenth-century apothecary, however, not only dispensed medicine but prescribed it, and knew how to use the surgical tools at his side. Dr. William Pasteur had an apothecary shop here in 1760. Fifteen years later he took into partnership a promising young surgeon, John Minson Galt, who had received his medical training in Edinburgh and London. The room at the rear of the shop was used as an office by the two doctors. Later Galt won honors as a field surgeon during the Revolution. The simulated stone facing which fronts the building, known as rustication, was an artificiality which appealed to some in colonial times when building stone was difficult and expensive to obtain.

Scrivener House-N. Reconstructed. Although one of Williamsburg's smaller buildings, this house characteristically retains the same scale as its larger neighbors in cornice, window, door, chimney,

and other details. This creates what one architect describes as "a happy feeling of pretension" for the householder of modest means. The building has been reconstructed from a photograph taken before the house was destroyed. From 1762 until 1772 a store was conducted here by Joseph Scrivener, whose diversified inventory included West India goods (rum, sugar, molasses, coffee, and ginger), oriental wares (tea, pepper, and allspice), Spanish and Portuguese commodities (wine, vinegar, and salt). The personal effects listed were largely of British manufacture. Privately occupied.

John Coke Office-S. Reconstructed. Little is known about the early history of the original building on this site. In the early 1800's it is believed to have served as the law office of a Williamsburg barrister, John Coke. Privately occupied.

Alexander Craig House-N. Restored. In 1771 a saddler named Alexander Craig purchased this frame residence. Earlier owners included an innkeeper, a glazier, and

a perukemaker. Like many other Williamsburg dwellings, the house grew in stages, but without losing its early individuality. Additions were made during the 1700's, the latest being the long shed roof at the rear. The space between the chimneys at the western end of the house was enclosed to provide closets. A formal pleasure garden with topiary work in box fronts on the street, affording a view of the outbuildings. The kitchen garden is beyond. Original brick is incorporated in the walks. Privately occupied.

Alexander Purdie House–S. Reconstructed. In 1767 this property was bought by Alexander Purdie, printer, at that time co-editor of Dixon's *Virginia Gazette.* He later established his own newspaper and printing office at Tarpley's store near by. The

versatile Purdie not only lived in the house, but operated a store here, selling millinery, jewelry, men's stockings, and — on one occasion — a second-hand, London-made phaeton with proper harness. Near the end of the century the house was briefly occupied by Cyrus Griffin, in 1788 President of Congress under the Articles of Confederation. Rebuilt on the exact lines of the old foundation, it is now connected by a concealed passageway to the King's Arms next door, and forms part of the restaurant operated there by Colonial Williamsburg. The outbuildings are grouped around a paved court; beyond this the formal garden, stable, and paddock run back to Francis Street.

King's Arms Tavern–S. Reconstructed. Now a public restaurant operated by Colonial Williamsburg, this inn still caters to the appetite as well as the eye of the guest. Jane Vobe operated here one of the most genteel taverns in the city, with a clientele which included William Byrd III, Sir Peyton Skipwith, and George Wash-

ington. Today, paneling and handsome furnishings of eighteenth-century design lend an air of hospitality and comfort. A wine vault rivals its colonial predecessor. The gambrel roof is given an interesting texture by the shingles with curved butts which were commonly used in Williamsburg. (Their purpose, however, was utilitarian rather than decorative. Square-ended shingles tend to warp and curl when dried out quickly in the hot Virginia sun.) At the rear of the tavern is an elaborate garden, in which meals are also served, weather permitting. The King's Arms has thus been reconstructed to belie the dictum of an outraged eighteenth-century gourmet: "Heaven sends good Meat, But the Devil sends Cooks!" Specialties are Virginia ham, fried chicken, escaloped oysters, Sally Lunn bread, and other traditional Southern dishes. Many of these are cooked from time-tested recipes of colonial days, as printed in *The Williamsburg Art of Cookery*.

Food in early Williamsburg was usually plentiful, even for those of limited means. Calory-counting was still unheard-of, although the medicinal qualities of some dishes were "recognized" by doctor and patient alike; one cookbook was entitled *A Collection of Receipts in Cookery, Physick, and Surgery: For the Use of all Good Wives, Tender Mothers, and Careful Nurses*. Appetites were prodigious in this bygone century and it was not unusual for the menu to include two "main courses," each consisting of a choice of eleven to fifteen dishes, with dessert to follow. Meals were customarily washed down with a tankard or more of beer.

The King's Arms, although outranked in historical fame by the Raleigh Tavern, has many associations with the past. In 1777 the Ohio Company of Virginia, then pressing its great land claims in the west, met here. During the Revolution, when Mrs. Vobe supplied food and drink to American troops, the energetic Baron Steuben ran up a bill of nearly three hundred dollars for lodging, board, and drinks. After the Revolution the King's Arms was renamed Eagle Tavern, in keeping with the spirit of independence in the new republic.

King's Arms Barber Shop – S. Reconstructed. Here, in another of Williamsburg's craft shops open to the public, a perukemaker patiently awaits the vanished trade of two centuries ago. Basin, razor, and soap dish rest beside a chromeless colonial barber chair. Close by is the cone-shaped mask which a gentleman clapped firmly over his face to allow him to breathe while the barber powdered his wig. A lady's wig, or hair, was dressed at home. Materials are at hand to fashion wigs of every description, and there are tools to curl and care for them. Since the barber of those days also performed minor dental and surgical operations, the shop is equipped with iron tooth-extractors and basins convenient for bloodletting.

Raleigh Tavern

Situated on the north side of Duke of Gloucester Street at the center of the busiest block in Williamsburg, the many-dormered Raleigh stood firmly in the foreground of life in the colonial capital. Most famous of Williamsburg hostelries, it was appropriately dedicated to Sir Walter Raleigh, who took a leading part in sending colonists to the new world and in encouraging the use of tobacco in England. A leaden bust of Sir Walter adorns the main doorway of the reconstructed tavern, one of the Exhibition Buildings of Colonial Williamsburg.

During all the year, but most particularly at Public Times, the Raleigh was a center of social activity. Balls held in its Apollo Room were second in elegance only to those in the Governor's Palace itself. Planters and merchants gathered at its bar to exchange news. Sturdy tavern tables were scarred by diceboxes as fortunes changed hands during the course of an evening. Tobacco smoke from long clay pipes filled the air, together with heated political discussions. Good-fellowship was sealed by a toast of Madeira or hot rum punch, or a pint of ale drunk from a pewter tankard.

George Washington, although he generally stopped elsewhere, often noted in his diary that he "dined at the Raleigh." After one evening of revelry in the year 1763, Thomas Jefferson, then a red-haired student at the College of William and Mary, complained in a letter to John Page: "Last night, as merry as agreeable company and dancing with *Belinda* in the *Apollo* could make me, I never could have thought the succeeding Sun would have seen me so wretched as I now am!"

Public receptions were common. In 1775, the Williamsburg Volunteers met here in honor of Peyton Randolph's return from Philadelphia, where he had served as first president of the Continental Congress. The following year, when Williamsburg troops heard that Patrick Henry, their Commander-in-Chief, was about to leave them, a dinner was given here in his honor. When the Treaty of Paris, ending the Revolution, was proclaimed in the city, the citizens of the new republic appropriately concluded their triumphal parade by a celebration at their principal tavern. Lafayette was welcomed on his return to Williamsburg in 1824 by a banquet in the Apollo, attended by the Governor and Council and by many notables including John Marshall and John C. Calhoun. Perhaps the last great reception held in the old Raleigh was in 1859, when the "fair and accomplished ladies of Williamsburg" arranged a banquet for alumni of the College—including former President Tyler. In December of that year the hostelry was leveled by fire.

The Raleigh was a center of business activity and the scene of many public auctions. Land, slaves, and goods were bought and sold "before the door of the Raleigh." In 1772, one merchant advertised: "I now have got a store Exactly opposite the Raleigh Tavern, which I look on as the best Situation in Williamsburg." The Raleigh also ranked with the Printing Office as a postal and news center: mail to go by sea was dispatched here, and newly arrived guests often served as the most effective "newspapers" of the day.

The aroused colonists met at the Raleigh to discuss grievances against the arbitrary policies of King and Parliament. When Governor Botetourt dissolved the Assembly in 1769 because of its protest against the British Revenue Act, the indignant burgesses reconvened at the Tavern to draw up a boycott of British goods. Five years later, other nonimportation measures were agreed upon at the Raleigh after the shocking news reached Virginia that Britain had ordered the port of Boston closed.

Two additional important meetings at the Raleigh foreshadowed

American independence. In 1773, five patriots gathered secretly here to weigh the need for closer co-operation among all the colonies in the growing dispute with England: Thomas Jefferson, his brother-in-law Dabney Carr, Patrick Henry, and the talented brothers Richard Henry Lee and Francis Lightfoot Lee. "Not thinking our old & leading members up to the point of forwardness & zeal which the times required," as Jefferson wrote, these rebellious burgesses organized Virginia's Committee of Correspondence. The following year "representatives of the people" met at the Raleigh to issue the call for the first Continental Congress.

Architects who reconstructed the Tavern were aided by two wood engravings made by Benson J. Lossing in 1848, by insurance policies, and by archaeological findings which revealed most of the original foundations of the building and many colonial artifacts. The furnishing of the Raleigh was guided by the painstaking inventories of early proprietors. After the death of Anthony Hay in 1771, every article in the Tavern was listed. Hay was also a noted cabinet-maker and doubtless took pleasure in making the elegance of his establishment equal to its reputation.

The Raleigh therefore stands again as it was in the days when Henry Wetherburn dispensed arrack punch—a brew so famous that on one occasion William Randolph of Tuckahoe sold two hundred acres of land in Goochland County to Peter Jefferson, father of Thomas, in consideration of Wetherburn's "biggest bowl of Arrack punch." The gentlemen of colonial Virginia and their ladies would find little change if they returned to dance again their minuets, and charter members of the Phi Beta Kappa Society, founded in Williamsburg in 1776, could again meet in the Apollo Room. The Raleigh's pervasive spirit of hospitality is well expressed in the motto gilded over the Apollo Room mantel: *Hilaritas Sapientiae et Bonae Vitae Proles*—"Jollity, the offspring of wisdom and good living."

Site of The Unicorn's Horn and John Carter's Store–N. In 1765 two brothers erected a brick building in this excellent business location one door west of Raleigh Tavern. John Carter owned the eastern half where he kept a store until his death in 1792. Dr. James Carter moved his apothecary shop, The Unicorn's Horn, into the other half. A third brother, Dr. William Carter, joined him, and after 1779 took over the business. The building was destroyed by fire the night the Raleigh burned in 1859.

Charlton House–S. Restored. This is a typical two-story Williamsburg house, with central entrance and a chimney at each end, in which simplicity of design is relieved by enrichment of detail in cornices and moldings. It was once the home and shop of Edward Charlton, an English wigmaker turned merchant, whose wares included such diverse items as cutlery, Queen's china (named after Queen Charlotte), horses, cows, harness, and books. In 1779, when Charlton

returned to England on a visit, he deeded the property to the widow and three children of his brother Richard, a tavern keeper, who had recently died. Privately occupied.

James Craig House–N. Reconstructed. The original house

on this site, probably erected before 1724, was torn down in 1907. Surviving photographs and firsthand descriptions made possible an accurate reconstruction. The house was purchased in 1765-66 by James Craig, a jeweler and silversmith. An "eminent Hand" at watchmaking assisted Craig at his shop, which was called the Golden Ball according to a notice in the *Virginia Gazette* in 1772. Privately occupied.

The Golden Ball–N. Restored. Buildings belonging to the merchant firm of Harmer and King stood on this site by 1745. This small brick storehouse which has survived was variously used thereafter, being probably at one time an apothecary shop. Later still it was occupied by Margaret Hunter and her sister Jane, both milliners. The building, like many others planned for commercial use, is placed with its gable end toward the street. The brick, original except for necessary patching, is laid in Flemish

bond. Now restored to its early appearance, the building houses the workshop of a pewterer and silversmith who fashions his wares with the same tools and painstaking skill as an eighteenth-century craftsman. In colonial days silver was a luxury and china, being imported, by no means a cheap commodity; pewter therefore served a wide variety of household needs. Its luster when well polished rivals that of silver, copper, and brass, and it can safely be used for food, because it is an alloy made almost entirely of tin. The Golden Ball, the name used for the shop of James Craig, jeweler and metalsmith who lived just east of here, has been adopted for this craft shop which is open to the public.

Russell House and William Randolph Lodging – N. Reconstructed. After occupancy by a merchant, apothecary, and milliner, the house on this site became in 1774 the home of one William Russell. It resembles many other small Williamsburg houses, but

eighteenth-century builders varied the use of individual elements of design in ways which lend character to the street scene as a whole. Here the treatment of the entrance to one side does not destroy the essential symmetry. At the extreme rear of the lot, on Nicholson Street, an unusual, narrow building has been reconstructed which is known as the William Randolph Lodging. It was the Williamsburg residence of William Randolph, a member of the Governor's Council and brother of Sir John Randolph. Both houses are privately occupied.

Bland-Wetherburn House – S. Richard Bland, a prominent colonial patriot, is believed to have been born here in 1710. The house is privately owned and has not been restored by Colonial Williamsburg. Bland, a prolific pamphleteer described by a contemporary as "staunch and tough as whitleather," formulated the concept of Britain's colonies as autonomous, linked to the Mother Country only through allegiance to the Crown—a concept ultimately borne out in our own day in the British Commonwealth of Nations. During most of the eighteenth century, the house was a tavern; Henry Wetherburn, previously host at the Raleigh, was the most famous proprietor. As at the Raleigh, important rooms were known by name, among them the End Room, the Bull's Head, and the Wheat Room.

Tarpley's Store-S. Reconstructed. The unusual front entrances reflect the joint use of this building as shop and residence. It is named for James Tarpley, a merchant, who in 1761 presented to

Bruton Church the bell—in use ever since—which is known as "Virginia's Liberty Bell" because it rang out the news of independence to Williamsburg's citizens. In 1775 Alexander Purdie acquired the property, which he used, until his death in 1779, as headquarters for his new *Virginia Gazette*—a rival to that published by Dixon and Hunter. For a short time prior to the Revolution there were three different papers of the same name issued in Williamsburg, all weeklies. Purdie took as his motto "Always for Liberty and the Public Good." At his printing shop he also sold books, stationery, and music for the harpsichord and violin. A privately operated shop.

Prentis House-N. Reconstructed. Archaeological excavations were particularly helpful in recreating this house. The foundations were unusually well preserved and the positions of brick walls and fence posts clearly indicated. From this evidence it was possible to establish the location of the front fence which extends beyond the

building line, an encroachment uncommon in Williamsburg. From Botetourt Street there is a good view of the outbuildings — the flanking storehouse and kitchen, the dairy, smokehouse, wellhead, and stable. Mary Brooke, wife of a prosperous merchant, William Prentis, inherited the property

from her father, John Brooke, who had built a house on the site between 1712 and 1714. It remained in the Prentis family until close to the end of the century. The diary and planting lists of a member of the family who grew up here were used in re-establishing the neatly fenced and formalized gardens. Privately occupied.

INTERSECTION OF BOTETOURT STREET

Davidson Shop–N. Reconstructed. Here was the apothecary  shop of Robert Davidson, a "Practitioner in Physick" and mayor of Williamsburg in 1738. Davidson's clients bought "Balsams, Decoctions, Electuaries, Elixirs, Emplaisters, Extracts, Infusions, Liquors, Magisteries, Oils, Ointments," and other remedies believed to soothe their ailments. The structure varies from the usual shop form in which the gable faces the street. Here a deep cornice protects the windows. A privately operated shop.

Waters-Coleman House–N. Reconstructed. Henry Gill built the original house on this lot soon after 1707, and operated an ordinary here. Later owners were Robert Davidson the apothecary,  and John Holt, who kept a store. Holt mortgaged the property in 1753 to Peyton Randolph and, being unable to meet the payments, lost it. The following year William Waters, gentleman, owner of several plantations and many slaves, bought it for a town house. About 1803, after the death of Waters and his widow, it was purchased by William Coleman, whose family continued to own it until the Civil War. Coleman, like Davidson and Holt before him, served as mayor of Williamsburg. Privately occupied.

Brick House Tavern–S. Reconstructed. Dr. William Carter, a leading businessman as well as surgeon and apothecary, acquired this property in 1761. He divided the building, selling part of it and renting the remainder. The multiple use is reflected in the six entrances. One proprietress advertised "12 or 14 very good lodging rooms, with fire places  to most of them." Gentlemen slept on the upper floor, ladies on the first floor. The corner room provided a choice location for a shopkeeper. Margaret Hunter ran a "Millinery Business in all its Branches" here in 1771, and also sold toys, cloaks, fans, and Scotch snuff. Very full records were found of the building, including a detailed plan drawn to scale. The brickwork is noteworthy; like all bricks used in the restoration, these have been molded by hand and baked in a kiln exactly as done in colonial days. The small wooden building behind is a reconstruction of a shop operated in 1766 by a riding-chair maker. The tavern is appropriately operated today as an adjunct of Williamsburg Lodge.

James Anderson House – S. Reconstructed. Between 1755 and 1760 the original house was owned by William Withers, secretary to Governor Dinwiddie. Thereafter it was for some years operated

as a tavern by Mrs. Christianna Campbell. It was here that George Washington frequently put up when he came to Williamsburg to attend the sessions as a member of the House of Burgesses, representing first Frederick and then Fairfax County. In 1770 a blacksmith, James Anderson, purchased the property and set up his forge in the rear. During the Revolution Anderson served as Public Armorer of Virginia. His daughter Nancy Camp inherited the house, and a description of it in an insurance policy taken out in her name aided the architects in the reconstruction. In 1842 the original house was destroyed in the disastrous fire which leveled practically all the buildings in this block. Privately occupied.

Teterel Shop – N. Reconstructed. A shop erected here late in the eighteenth century has been reconstructed with the aid of a measured drawing attached to an insurance policy taken out by Francis Teterel in 1806. Teterel occupied the shop from 1802 to 1823. It has familiar shop features— the gable end facing the street and the two display windows. The hood projecting from the face of the building is designed to shelter prospective customers from heat or inclement weather.

A privately operated shop.

Mary Stith Shop–S. Reconstructed. This small brick building, referred to as "Wood's shop," was the property of Mary Stith, daughter of the distinguished historian, the Reverend Dr. William Stith, President of the College. She would seem to have enjoyed a comfortable living, possibly augmented by the rent for the shop, for in 1792 she owned four slaves, and in 1815 possessed "calico curtains, 5 bedsteads, 5 chests of drawers, 1 cloathes press, 2 tables, [and a] Pianoforte." In her will she freed her slaves and left her

property to them to recompense their services. Privately occupied.

Virginia Gazette Printing Office Site–N. Here stood the printing establishment of William Parks, by appointment "Public Printer" of Virginia and founder of the earliest newspaper in the Virginia colony. On August 6, 1736, the first issue of the *Virginia Gazette* came off his press. The files of this weekly offer present-day readers a lively account of the life of colonial America; they have also supplied much information of use in the restoration of Williamsburg. The discriminating typography of Parks is evident in the newspaper, as well as in the laws of the colony and other books which he published. He is remembered also for the establishment of a paper mill just outside Williamsburg—"the first Mill of the Kind, that ever was erected in this Colony." In this venture he had the advice and backing of a fellow printer, Benjamin Franklin, who later purchased paper from the mill. After Parks' death his daughter — Patrick Henry's mother-in-law — sold the property to William Hunter, who continued publication of the *Gazette* until his death in 1762; Hunter's son being then a minor, the paper was carried on by Joseph Royle, who died in 1766, and then by John Dixon and Alexander Purdie. Later Purdie established his own paper, and Dixon was joined by young William Hunter. Hunter, a Loyalist, supplied the British with military information and fought with Cornwallis at Yorktown; in consequence his property was confiscated at the war's end. During excavation at this site several hundred pieces of type, probably of Dutch origin, were unearthed, along with a bookbinder's ornament and crucibles which Parks may have used to melt lead for this type. The site is privately owned.

Orlando Jones House and Office–S. Reconstructed. The T-shaped chimneys and porch chamber to the rear of the house identify this gable-roofed structure with the first quarter of the eighteenth century. Orlando Jones, who owned the original house prior to his death in 1719, was the son of the Reverend Rowland Jones, first rector of Bruton Parish. Orlando Jones, born in 1681, became a landowner in York and King William counties, and several times represented the latter in the House of Burgesses. His daughter, Frances, and her husband, John Dandridge, were the parents of Martha Washington. The oval garden departs from the usual square or rectangular layout. Box hedges, corner seats, and crape myrtle accent the design, and a gnarled paper-mulberry tree provides summer shade. The word "office" in colonial days was applied to any small subsidiary building not otherwise designated as to use. Both buildings are guesthouses for Williamsburg Inn.

Pitt-Dixon House and The Sign of the Rhinoceros–N. Reconstructed. Like the residence of Orlando Jones across the street, this building is an example of the most common colonial house form in Williamsburg. A shed roof at the rear covers additional first-floor space. Wooden grilles at the basement openings are characteristic, although the location of the kitchen in the basement is uncommon. Built about 1717-19, the original house had as an early owner Christopher de Graffenreid, son of the celebrated Swiss baron who deserted the courts of Charles II and Louis XIV to found New Bern, North Carolina. Later the young widow Sarah Packe kept a

millinery shop here and took in lodgers— among whom, in 1746, was Edmund Pendleton, destined to become a Revolutionary leader. Sarah Packe soon after married George Pitt who opened an apothecary shop, The Sign of the Rhinoceros, on the property. Visitors who walk a few steps under the arching live oaks of Colonial Street will see the curved shop window of a small building, the handsome cornice of which echoes that of the main house. Pitt sold the property to the printer John Dixon in 1774. Both buildings are privately occupied.

INTERSECTION OF COLONIAL STREET

Archibald Blair's Storehouse – N. Restored. This building, a garage before its restoration, is one of Williamsburg's best examples of shop architecture. Erected about 1715, it was part of a larger building used by Archibald Blair as a storehouse. The original brick-

work was revealed after the painstaking removal of numerous coats of paint. Blair, who combined the roles of physician and successful merchant, left the building to his son John Blair, and it was occupied by the firm of Prentis & Company in which John was a partner. It was to this firm that the shipment of tea was consigned which Yorktown patriots dumped into the York River in their own "tea-party" of 1774. Today the building houses a printing office; inside a master printer again minds that his p's and q's are not mixed in his

type case. He commands two presses — one original and one an accurate reproduction. Using old-style Caslon type, he sets his work in the eighteenth-century manner. He locks his forms in an old-fashioned chase. His ink is hand-mixed from varnish and lamp-black.

and he prints on laid paper resembling that used by Williamsburg's early printers. Eleven hand operations are required to print a single sheet; with his assistant, the colonial printer could print only about 240 sheets in an hour—one reason why most newspapers were weeklies. This craft shop, open to the public, does custom printing, and also sells quill pens, souvenir printing, paper, and books.

Captain Orr's Dwelling–S. Partially restored. Erected sometime before 1743, this simple but comfortable dwelling has stood through the centuries with little change. The rear cornice has a two-foot overhang which makes a wider roof and thus adds needed space to the second floor. Another pleasing irregularity of this familiar over-all house design is the placing of one of the end chimneys inside the house, the other outside. Early in the 1920's, one elderly resident of Williamsburg recalled that here she had helped to prepare food for the Confederate army retreating before McClellan. "On the day the battle of Williamsburg was fought, I stood before this house all day passing out biscuits and meat to our men." The house was originally owned by a blacksmith, Hugh  Orr. In those days a craftsman in Williamsburg had excellent opportunities for marketing his wares to the visiting gentry as well as the townspeople. Although Orr encountered financial difficulties early in his career, his skill and hard work had enabled him, by the time of his death in 1764, to amass a comfortable estate. Items in the inventory suggest that material prosperity also brought social and intellectual advancement. Orr owned a library of about forty books, many of which indicated a broadminded approach to one of the major intellectual controversies of the day: there were four volumes by the Anglican theologian Dean Prideaux, and three volumes of *The Free Thinker*. Wine glasses, a silver teapot, six "Views with gilt frames," and thirteen tablecloths point to a certain ease of living. Orr bore the title of captain in the Williamsburg militia, but his tombstone in Bruton churchyard bears only the modest designation "Hammer Man," proclaiming his pride of craft. Privately occupied.

Ludwell-Paradise House

Erected between 1700 and 1717, this handsome brick mansion on the north side of Duke of Gloucester Street was architecturally sophisticated and advanced for its day. Originally the town house of the prominent Ludwell family, it has been restored as an Exhibition Building of Colonial Williamsburg and today houses a unique and comprehensive collection of American Folk Art, gathered and presented to Colonial Williamsburg by Mrs. John D. Rockefeller, Jr.

The house was built by Philip Ludwell II as a family residence during Public Times, when political duties brought him to the capital. Ludwell, who also owned a magnificent estate, Green Spring, near by, held a succession of important offices. In 1695, at the age of twenty-three, he was elected speaker of the House of Burgesses, probably the youngest man ever to be given this responsibility. Later he was a councilor and Auditor of the Colony. Ludwell was a political opponent of Governor Spotswood, and his Williamsburg home was probably a meeting place for those who shared his convictions. On his death in 1727, the house and other property passed to his son, Philip Ludwell III, who also became a burgess and member of the Council.

Occupancy of the house ultimately devolved to Lucy, second daughter of Philip Ludwell III, although she never owned it. This eccentric lady lived most of her life in London. Her husband, John Paradise, a scholar and linguist, was a member of Dr. Samuel Johnson's charmed circle of literati. Lucy Paradise startled London society by such exploits as dashing boiling water from her tea urn on a too garrulous gentleman who annoyed her. Because of her residence in England, property which she owned in Virginia was confiscated by the Commonwealth during the Revolution, prompting Dr. Johnson to refer to it as "Paradise's Loss."

In 1805, ten years after her husband's death, Mrs. Paradise returned to take up residence in the house built by her grandfather. Her peculiarities eventually became so marked that she was committed to the state asylum. One of her capricious customs was to entertain callers in a coach which had been reassembled inside the house, and was rolled to and fro by a servant during these visits.

Apparently the house was originally intended, like the George Wythe and Allen-Byrd houses, to have a second floor as wide as the first, with four full rooms; the builders, however, changed their plans and reduced this depth by one half, covering the rear portion of the first floor by a shed roof. Little repair work was needed to restore the building to its early appearance. The brickwork, a fine example of Flemish bond with headers laid in a pattern, was found to be in excellent condition. In the basement may be seen the original exposed framing of massive pieces of hand-hewn timber. This was the first property acquired by Mr. Rockefeller and Dr. Goodwin for restoration.

A garden, prized for its dwarf box collection, links the house to the stable and paddock on Nicholson Street. The planting stresses holly, spring bulbs, and summer flowering shrubs. Outbuildings include a well, smokehouse, and necessary house, with a wood house handy to the kitchen.

Most of the examples of folk art shown here belong to the nineteenth century rather than the eighteenth. Folk art flourished in the period just following the Revolution; the industrial age caused a decline in the efforts of self-taught artists.

Lightfoot House and Kitchen–S. Colonel Philip Lightfoot, a wealthy Yorktown merchant and planter, owned this property early in the eighteenth century. The building with the clipped gambrel roof was a kitchen used also as an office; it is reconstructed. The house, to the west, is original and contains a beautifully executed stairway. Colonel Lightfoot was appointed to the Governor's Council in 1733. In addition to this house, where he entertained his friends when business or politics brought him to Williamsburg, he owned plantations in seven counties, 180 slaves, a "four wheeled and two wheeled Chaise," and a "coach and six horses." On his death in 1748 Lightfoot bequeathed £500 to establish the Lightfoot Foundation, a scholarship at the College of William and Mary for "two poor scholars forever to be brought up to the Ministry of the Church of Eng-

land or such other publick employment as shall be most suitable to their capacitys." The property remained in the Lightfoot family until 1839. Both buildings are privately occupied.

Blair's Brick House–N. Reconstructed. Clipped gables, often seen in Tidewater Virginia, accentuate the robust outside chimneys of this house and add greatly to the beauty of the roof

lines. The checkerboard pattern in glazed brick is associated with the early 1700's; the use of rubbed brick to emphasize the structural elements of the walls is here fully exemplified. A basement kitchen is a feature of the house established by unusually complete archaeological evidence. The site, once thought to have been among the holdings of John Blair, Sr., is now known to have been one of the three lots granted in 1700 to Philip Ludwell. In 1770 Lucy

Paradise received the property, then designated as the "Red Lyon," as part of her inheritance from her father, Philip Ludwell II. The garden, open to the public, has a sunken turf panel with corner seats, a pleached alley, and an aerial hedge of clipped live oaks; it is shaded by tall locusts. A privately operated shop.

Peter Hay's Shop–S. Reconstructed. In 1746 Dr. Peter Hay advertised his apothecary shop "adjoining the Market-Place." Ten years later a notice in the *Maryland Gazette* reported that in Williamsburg "On Sunday last betwixt one and two o'Clock in the Day, a Fire broke out in the Shop of Dr. Peter Hay . . . and in less than Half an Hour entirely consumed the same, together with all Medicines, Utensils, &c. . . . and by the Assistance of a Fire Engine, it was happily prevented from doing any further Damage." Excavations on the site revealed a large chimney foundation and some fragments thought to be the "Utensils" mentioned above. Privately occupied.

Intersection of Queen Street

Chowning's Tavern–N. Reconstructed. In function as in appearance Chowning's Tavern again takes its place in Williamsburg. Not only has it been rebuilt to resemble its eighteenth-century predecessor, but it is today operated by Colonial Williamsburg as an alehouse of two centuries ago. Its specialties include Brunswick stew, pecan waffles, Welsh rabbit, oysters, clams, "sallad," and sandwiches made from thick slices of French bread. Draft ale and beer, wines and spiced punch are also served.

In 1766 Josiah Chowning (pronounced Chewning) advertised the opening of his tavern "where all who please to favour me with their Custom may depend upon the best of Entertainment for Themselves, Servants, and Horses, and good Pasturage." The rates which could be charged for each item on the bill of fare were duly fixed each year by the justices of the county, and were ordered to be "openly set up in the common entertaining room."

Chowning's Tavern served a less august clientele than the Raleigh or the King's Arms, and today's furnishings were selected accordingly. The sturdy, country-made tables and the Windsor and ladder-back chairs are such as might have been found in a tavern of this sort. Pewter plates, tankards, and measures, which would have formed part of the tavern's equipment, decorate the candle-lit rooms, and on the walls, sporting prints and cartoons of the time are hung.

When weather permits, guests are served in the yard behind the tavern, shaded by an arbor of scuppernong grapes. Colonial statutes were explicit in stating that all licensing laws were equally binding out of doors in "booths, arbours and stalls." Taverns often provided outdoor amusements also; here there are horseshoe pits in a small enclosure. The kitchen, dairy, and smokehouse have been reconstructed on their original sites in the yard. In the rear of the lot, where eighteenth-century travelers found pasturage for their horses, visitors of today are invited to leave their cars. This is one of several parking spaces provided in the restored area.

Market Square Tavern–S. Restored. In intermittent use as a hostelry during three centuries, the Market Square Tavern is today operated in the same capacity by Williamsburg Lodge. Its most celebrated colonial proprietor was Gabriel Maupin, who acquired the property in 1771. Maupin also served as Keeper of the Magazine— conveniently located next door — and conducted a saddlery and harnessmaker's business. In 1775, Maupin christened his son George

Washington, a custom soon to be followed by thousands of his countrymen. The building offers a good example of the way in which many colonial structures gracefully "grew" over the years by means of frequent additions. The eastern portion is the earliest and contains a handsome "Great Room" which is completely sheathed and paneled with the original pine in natural finish. The kitchen yard played an important part as a work area, and the garden provided a meeting place for games and sociability. The coach house and paddock in the rear no longer provide quarters for blooded coach horses, but the Tavern's garden, with its fruit trees, flowers, and herbs, is open to the public and is still favored by Williamsburg visitors as a place of relaxation.

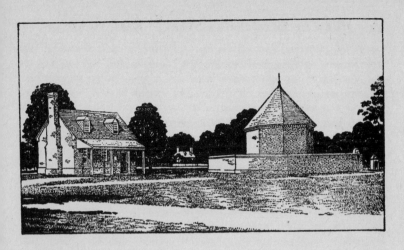

The Magazine and Guardhouse

A sturdy octagonal building, standing apart in the green expanse of Market Square, the Magazine was the forerunner of today's labyrinthine arsenals. It was erected in 1715 on the urgent request of Governor Alexander Spotswood for a "substantial" brick building to house the arms and ammunition dispatched from the Tower of London by order of Queen Anne for the defense of the royal colony. The Governor himself is credited with the design. Sir William Keith, Governor of Pennsylvania, who visited Williamsburg, wrote in 1738 that Spotswood "was well acquainted with Figures, and so good a Mathematician, that his Skill in Architecture . . . is yet to be seen in *Virginia,* by the Building of an elegant safe Magazine." The structure has survived to the present day and is now an Exhibition Building of Colonial Williamsburg.

In colonial times, the Magazine provided an adequate storehouse for the military needs of Virginia. The first line of defense of the colony was the Royal Navy, which regularly convoyed the annual tobacco fleet and maintained one or more men-of-war on the "Virginia Station" in time of stress. But against Indian attacks, local riots, slave insurrections, or even raids from pirates or enemy privateers, the colony depended for its defense upon the periodic military service of its inhabitants. Then as now, the protection of hearth and home was recognized as the duty of every freeman. With the exception of clergymen, Quakers, schoolmasters, ferrymen, pilots, overseers, and government officials, every able-bodied freeman from sixteen to sixty was obliged by law to serve in the local militia, under command of the leading gentlemen of the county whom the governor commissioned as officers.

The Magazine assumed added importance during the French and Indian War (1754-63) when the colony for the first time conducted large-scale military operations on its own soil—the Ohio Valley. At this time, the amount of gunpowder to be stored having reached sixty thousand pounds, the people of Williamsburg felt that the Magazine needed further protection. A high wall was accordingly built around it, and provision made for a guard. A guardhouse was built close by. The wall and the Guardhouse, pulled down in the nineteenth century, were reconstructed with the aid of archaeological findings and surviving water-color sketches made in the early 1800's.

It was during the night of April 20-21, 1775, that the Magazine played its most dramatic role in an incident which did much to precipitate the Revolution in Virginia. In the preceding month the Second Virginia Convention had met in Richmond and had passed a bill for the assembling and training of the militia. At this gathering Patrick Henry made the famous declaration: "Is life so dear, or peace so sweet, as to be purchased at the price of chains and slavery? Forbid it, Almighty God! I know not what course others may take, but as for me, give me liberty or give me death."

In Williamsburg Lord Dunmore deemed it wise to have a supply of powder removed from the Magazine, explaining in a letter to London that the action was taken in response to "The series of dangerous measures pursued by the people of this Colony against Government." His orders were carried out by a company of British marines under cover of darkness, but, as the Governor reported, "tho' it was intended to have been done privately, *Mr. Collins* and his party were observed, and Notice was given immediately to the Inhabitants of this Place; Drums were then sent thro' the City."

Public indignation rose to fever pitch and troops were mustered in various places. Patrick Henry led a party of armed volunteers toward the capital from Hanover, demanding return of the powder or payment for it. To this demand the Receiver-General of Virginia was constrained to yield; payment was duly made and the "rebels" dispersed. In somewhat injured tones, Governor Dunmore explained that his only intention had been to forestall the capture of the powder in "an intended insurrection of the slaves"; for this he "certainly rather deserved the thanks of the country than their reproaches." His proclamation, however, did little to calm public sentiment, and an uneasy quiet prevailed. Meanwhile, less than forty-eight hours before the removal of the powder, British troops had fired on Massachusetts irregulars at Lexington. When this news reached Williamsburg, eight days later, the *Virginia Gazette* proclaimed in a broadside "the sword is now drawn, and God knows when it will be sheathed."

After the Revolution there was no longer any need for an arsenal at Williamsburg, although the Magazine was pressed into service for powder storage once more by Confederate forces during the Civil War. In other years it was used variously as a market place, a Baptist meeting house, a dancing school, and finally as a livery stable.

The Magazine and Guardhouse have been equipped with weapons and furnishings of the period of the French and Indian War. The officer of the guard wears the uniform of the First Virginia Regiment—a unit organized and commanded by George Washington—which took a leading part in the war. The men on guard are not in uniform since they would have been furnished only with muskets and ammunition. Their chief sentry beat was made along the path fronting the sentry box, itself carefully modeled from military handbooks of the day.

Within the Magazine military equipment of the eighteenth century is exhibited, including a collection of flintlock muskets—the standard arm of all British and colonial troops. On the bench in the Armorer's Workshop parts of a typical musket of the 1750's are shown disassembled, together with the armorer's tools. The reconstructed Guardhouse is a typical story-and-a-half brick structure, simply furnished. In the small, brick-paved room on the ground floor a few muskets are racked at one end and soldiers' accouterments are hung about the room.

The Association for the Preservation of Virginia Antiquities, chartered in 1889, made the safeguarding of the Magazine from almost certain ruin one of its first projects. The Association acquired the Magazine in 1890 and exhibited it for a number of years. In 1947 the A.P.V.A. leased the property to be restored and exhibited by Colonial Williamsburg.

Courthouse of 1770

At the center of the busy life of Market Square, a courthouse was erected in 1770 which has stood as a symbol of law and order for nearly two centuries. It served Williamsburg and James City County until superseded in 1932 by a new structure on South England Street. The restored building now houses the Archaeological Museum of Colonial Williamsburg and is open to the public without charge. Like many other Virginia courthouses, it is T-shaped. Arched windows and an octagonal cupola add to the official appearance of the building. The design of the overhanging pediment would seem to call for columns, but there is no documentary evidence of their having been ordered from England and the building is known to have stood without them until renovations were undertaken in 1911. When restoration work was carried out, it was therefore decided to leave this pediment just as it had been in the eighteenth century.

Two courts regularly met here—the James City County Court and the municipal court (known as the Court of Hustings). The county court was the principal unit of local government in colonial Virginia, possessed of wide powers, both judicial and executive. Its criminal jurisdiction was restricted to cases not involving "life or member," although an exception was made to allow it to prescribe ear-cropping for a culprit caught stealing a hog. The Court of Hustings was at first chiefly a court of record, although in the course of time it assumed the criminal and civil jurisdiction within the city which the county court exercised elsewhere.

Both the inside and outside of the building have a place in history. Legal notices were posted in front of the Courthouse, and citizens gathered in excitement at its steps to hear announcements of importance. The Declaration of Independence was proclaimed here, to the roll of drums and the pealing of bells at the College, Church, and Capitol.

Market Square, the broad green on which the Courthouse is set, was an important center in community life, just as those who had planned the city intended. Militiamen were mustered here. Farmers from the countryside used it as a market place each Wednesday and Saturday. Twice during the year, on St. George's Day (April 23) and on December 12, a great official town fair was held at the square. Livestock was sold, as well as a bewildering array of other merchandise; there were games, puppet shows, cudgeling matches, beauty contests, cock fights, dancing and fiddling for prizes, and the familiar chase for "A Pig, with the Tail soap'd."

INTERSECTION OF ENGLAND STREET

Norton-Cole House – N. Partially restored. In this composite building the wing parallel to Duke of Gloucester Street is modern. The brick house, facing on the green of Market Square, was built about 1830 by Roscow Cole on the foundations of a colonial dwelling occupied in the 1770's by Dr. John Baker, a "surgeon dentist." Baker is considered to have made a notable contribution to the development of dentistry in America. Entries in George Washington's

ledger show numerous payments to Dr. Baker for professional services. John Hatley Norton of the London mercantile firm, John Norton & Sons, later lived here. Privately occupied.

Greenhow-Repiton House and Brick Office–S. Both the frame house (reconstructed) and the adjacent brick office (restored) were once the property of John Greenhow whose dwelling and store stood to the west. Greenhow, a

merchant in Williamsburg from about 1755 until his death in 1787, sold china to Patrick Henry for the Palace during Henry's residence there as first governor of the newborn commonwealth. The townspeople are reported to have complained of his high prices.

A somewhat unconventional appearance is given to this otherwise typical colonial dwelling by the shed-roof additions at the rear and to the east of the building. Reconstruction of the house— destroyed early in the present century—was aided by a water color and photographs. The brick office behind the house was known by local tradition as the Debtors' Prison, but there is no actual evidence of such use. The design and construction make it seem probable that it was used as a shop or residence in colonial days. In 1810 Joseph Repiton purchased all this property

from Greenhow's son. Both buildings are privately occupied.

Boot and Shoemaker's Shop–S. Reconstructed. Here a craftsman works at a sturdy cobbler's bench making and repairing shoes with the tools and techniques of the eighteenth century. Hanging on the wall is a collection of wooden lasts on which to shape the shoe leather. Well-to-do colonial customers had their own lasts which they left with the cobbler. Some of the soles were secured with wooden pegs, but for the most part they were hand-sewn with "good thread well twisted" and the stitches "hard drawn with handleathers," as the statutes prescribed. In colonial Virginia severe penalties were imposed for shoddy workmanship, or leather not properly tanned and curried. It was safer to order shoes made to measure at home than to risk ordering from abroad. So skilled did native shoemakers become that the wealthy William Nelson observed in 1770 that his "shoes, hose [and] buckles" were made in America, and that they "improve every year in quantity as well as quality."

Shoes of that period might not seem attractive today, however: fashion decreed square toes with no distinction between right and left and no fitting to the instep. The craft shop, operated by Colonial Williamsburg and open to the public, occupies the site of the shoemaking establishment of George Wilson & Co. In 1773 Wilson advertised "a choice Cargo of the best Sorts of English Leather for all Manner of Mens Shoes and Pumps, and excellent London Drawlegs for Boots."

Site of John Greenhow's House and Store–S. Here for many years stood Travis House, a restaurant operated by Colonial Williamsburg. It has been superseded by the King's Arms Tavern, near the Capitol. Travis House, though built in the eighteenth century, was not originally at this location and has therefore been moved. In colonial times the merchant John Greenhow lived on this site. A detailed description of a "wooden Dwelling and Store house" has been found in an insurance policy taken out by his son in 1801. This, with other evidence, will make possible the reconstruction of these original buildings.

James Geddy House–N. Restored. This unusual L-shaped house served as home and shop for James Geddy, a skilled gunsmith.

In 1737, Geddy announced that he sold guns "as cheap as they are usually sold in England." An inventory, made in 1744 shortly after his death, lists the molds, anvils, lathes, grindstones, and other tools of the gunmaker. Though not wealthy, Geddy was moderately well-to-do, leaving — among other property—three Negro slaves. His sons David and William carried on the gunsmith's trade, although they also stocked such general merchandise as "Rupture Bands of different Sorts" and "a Vermifuge . . . which safely and effectually destroys all Kinds of Worms in Horses." However, during most of the period until the Revolution the property was occupied by a third son, James Geddy, Jr., a goldsmith, silversmith, and jeweler. Young Geddy feared that his shop was too far from the Capitol, for he once advertised that the "Reasonableness" of his goods should "remove the Objection of his Shop's being too high up Town.'" The box garden bordering Palace Green is open to the public. The house is privately occupied.

INTERSECTION OF PALACE GREEN

Custis-Maupin House–S. Reconstructed. John Custis owned the original of this house, or tenement, as a "house to rent" was called in the eighteenth century. Various stages of growth are discernible: it was first enlarged by a one-and-one-half story wing to the west, then by another addition behind that. This earlier house was replaced when, about 1840, John M. Maupin built a "handsome house on the site of an old ruinous building opposite the lower corner of the churchyard." Privately occupied.

James Galt House–S. Restored. James Galt—brother of John Minson Galt who practiced medicine at what is now called the Pasteur-Galt Apothecary Shop—for a while followed his father's calling of gold and silversmith and watchmaker. He became keeper of the "Lunatick Hospital" when it opened in 1773, remaining until his death in 1800, except for the years he served as a lieutenant of militia during the Revolution. According to a contemporary, he performed his duties as "a man of much humanity." His son, William T. Galt, succeeded him. The colonial cottage which bears James Galt's name was enlarged during the eighteenth century from an original one-room structure. It was later moved to this location from the grounds of Eastern State Hospital. The land on which it stands was deeded to John Custis in 1717 and it is probable that Custis built and rented a house here, as he did on adjoining lots. To allow excavations, the James Galt House will eventually be moved elsewhere. Privately occupied.

Bruton Parish Church

At the corner of Duke of Gloucester Street and Palace Green, Bruton Parish Church stands as a strong link between the past and the present. From the days when it was the court church for the colony to the present time it has been in continuous use. The building, a fine architectural example of the colonial church in America, is a reminder in bricks and mortar of the part religion played in the daily life of eighteenth-century Virginia. It was a rector of this parish, the late Reverend Dr. W. A. R. Goodwin, who first conceived the restoration of Williamsburg, and interested John D. Rockefeller, Jr., in the project. Together they shared the leadership and development of the work.

Bruton Parish was formed in 1674 by merging two earlier parishes (one of them founded in 1633); it was named for an English parish in Somerset from which several leading parishioners came, among them Thomas Ludwell and Colonel John Page. A new brick church was ordered built at Middle Plantation in 1677, on land given by Colonel Page. Completed in 1683, the small buttressed brick church in Jacobean style was big enough for a rural parish; with the establishment of the College and the removal of the capital from Jamestown to Williamsburg, however, it soon became inadequate. Accordingly, Governor Spotswood in 1711 presented the vestry with a "draught" for a new church and the Assembly appropriated £200 to help defray the cost. The present church was begun that year, close by the old, and was completed in 1715. The vestry set aside a large square pew for the use of the governor and his twelve councilors. The governor was also provided with a canopied chair. The transept pews during sessions of the Assembly were reserved for members of the House of Burgesses.

Church and State were united in colonial Virginia, and office-holders under the Crown were obliged to conform to the Established Church. All classes of colonists, from great planters to the humblest artisan and slave, participated in the sacraments of the Anglican Church and joined in its corporate worship. As the Virginia aristocracy was politically minded, most of the leading planters became members of the Assembly and, as such, worshipped in Bruton Church. According to the records, the stone font, believed to have been brought from Jamestown, witnessed the baptism of fourteen slaves for whom George Washington stood godfather. At times of political crisis, the aid of God was humbly sought: in 1774, when word reached Williamsburg that Parliament had closed the port of Boston, the burgesses set aside a day for fasting, humiliation, and prayer, and went to Bruton in a body "to implore the divine interposition, for averting the heavy Calamity which threatens destruction to our Civil Rights, and the Evils of civil War."

The chancel of the church, originally 25 feet shorter than today, was enlarged in 1752 to accommodate an organ from England. The first organist, who served for 43 years, was Peter Pelham, stepbrother of the Boston artist, John Singleton Copley. Since Pelham was also keeper of the Gaol, he habitually and conveniently brought a prisoner with him to pump the organ. The colonial organ, disposed of in 1840, has been replaced by one made by Green of London in 1785. The church also has a modern, three-manual Skinner organ.

The walls and windows of the church are original, but much of the interior woodwork was torn out during the nineteenth century; the old high pews were cut down, the colonial pulpit discarded, and the west end partitioned off as a Sunday School room. The Victorian taste of the 1880's was even responsible for the introduction of plush-bottomed, spurious Gothic chairs. The interior, partially restored in 1905, and more completely in 1938, once again resembles its eighteenth-century appearance.

The west gallery is original. It has long been known as Lord Dunmore's Gallery because of the tradition that the Governor worshiped there with his party for several Sundays before he fled Williamsburg. It was originally set aside for the use of students of the College, whose initials carved in the handrail are still discernible. The north transept gallery was used by slaves, and was at one time entered by an outside stairway. A pew in the south gallery was reserved for the speaker of the House of Burgesses, and a portion "nearer the Pulpit" designated for the faculty of the College.

It was considered an honor in colonial times to be buried within the confines of the church. Among the gravestones which can be seen there are those of the royal governor, Francis Fauquier—to whom Jefferson paid tribute as "the ablest man" who ever filled the office of governor; the great Virginia patriot, Edmund Pendleton; and the Reverend Rowland Jones, great-grandfather of Martha Washington and the first rector of the parish from 1674 until 1688.

The main portion of the church is symmetrical; chancel and nave are equal. The use of arched doors and both round and arched windows is typical of colonial churches in Virginia. The brick is a light salmon color, laid in Flemish bond, with glazed headers set in a checkerboard pattern. In 1769 a new tower was built employing the darker colored brick without glaze characteristic of the later period. The wall, capped by stout molded brick, which encloses the churchyard, dates from 1754. The roof of the church is steep, and the rake boards at the gables taper in width as they ascend the ridges, creating the impression of an even steeper pitch. This soaring quality is climaxed in the emphatic vertical of the tower, surmounted by the wooden steeple. Here hangs Virginia's Liberty Bell which rang out the news of the Declaration of Independence, the surrender of Cornwallis, and the signing of the peace treaty in 1783. Today it still sounds its invitation to worship.

Maupin Shop (Chamber of Commerce)–S. Restored. Now used as an office by the Chamber of Commerce, this early nineteenth-century building resembles many colonial shops in that its gable end faces the street, permitting spacious display windows.

Taliaferro - Cole Shop and Pulaski Club–S. Restored. Only the street front of this colonial shop required restoration; the work was simplified by the discovery of a water color, painted in 1834 by Millington, which showed the shop and the Taliaferro-Cole House. The distinctive and unusually long shed roof was extended far beyond the outer wall to shelter a near-by well. The shop was owned and probably built by Charles Taliaferro prior to 1782. In 1804 it was purchased by Jesse Cole

along with the house next door. He used the smaller building as an apothecary shop, post office, and general store. In 1827 a member of the College faculty wrote in wonderment that everything from "hams and French brandy" to "black silk stockings and shell oysters" could be found here. A plaque in front of the shop commemorates the Pulaski Club, an informal discussion group of long standing which still meets here. It was named for the Polish count who fought and died for American independence. The shop is privately operated.

Taliaferro-Cole House–S. Restored. Charles Taliaferro (pro-nounced Tolliver), well known both as coachmaker and merchant, is believed to have occupied this house soon after 1760. He also owned fourteen lots in Williamsburg, a large tract of land in the country, and a "brewhouse" and warehouse at College Landing, one of the two shallow-water "ports" of the city, on Archer's Hope

Creek. Among other activities, Taliaferro controlled several small,

flatbottomed river boats, manned by Negro crews, which were employed in coastal trade on the bay and river. In 1779, he offered for sale at the warehouse salt, tar, barreled pork, hogs' lard, bacon, shad and herring, coal, pine plank, and cypress boards. A census of 1783 noted that Taliaferro had eleven slaves, five horses, and four cattle. In 1804 the property was purchased by Jesse Cole, whose descendants occupied the house until recently. The house and outbuildings, which lie along Nassau Street, form an L, a general plan similar to that of the George Wythe property. The unusual front porch was reconstructed according to dimensions revealed by antique weatherboards. Privately occupied.

Intersection of Nassau Street

Bryan House—S. Reconstructed. The typical A-roof house built on this site about the middle of the 1700's survived until early in the present century, being used in the intervening years as a grocery store, residence, and school. It was owned at the end of the eighteenth century by a family named Bryan. The architects were guided in the work of reconstruction by a few photographs which were found, and by residents who recalled the appearance of the house. The garden, unusually placed at the side of the house, has  a formal arrangement of clipped box hedges and topiary work, and includes the customary fruit trees, as well as a handsome arbor and a sheltered bench. The garden is open to the public. The house is privately occupied.

Blaikley-Durfey House and Durfey Shop—S. Reconstructed. William Blaikley owned this lot as early as 1736, and his widow was living in a house here at the time of her death in 1771. According to the *Virginia Gazette* she was "an eminent Midwife . . . who, in the course of her Practice, brought upwards of three thousand Children into the World." In 1773 a tailor, Severinus Durfey, occupied the house and the second building is believed to have been his shop, where customers could "depend on their work being done in the best Manner." Privately occupied.

John Blair House – N. Restored. Here lived John Blair, Jr., scion of a distinguished Williamsburg family. His grandfather was Dr. Archibald Blair, and his granduncle was Dr. James Blair, able but hot-tempered founder of the College. Blair's father, John Blair, Sr.—who inherited a fortune said to have exceeded £10,000 from his uncle—was a burgess, later a councilor, and from 1728 until his death in 1771, Auditor-General of the Colony. He was twice acting governor of Virginia. John Blair, Jr., graduated from William and Mary, studied at the Middle Temple, London, and himself became a burgess and Clerk of the Council. He was on the committee which drew up Virginia's Declaration of Rights and first state constitution, and he served the new commonwealth as councilor, judge, and chief justice. In 1787, he represented Virginia at the Constitutional Convention, where he firmly advocated federal union. President Washington appointed him to the United States Supreme Court in 1789, where he served until his retirement to Williamsburg in 1796. He died in 1800. The house has the early type of hipped dormers, and the original stone steps which were imported from England. The kitchen, with its huge chimney, is reconstructed. Between the kitchen and the street is a small, formal herb garden. Both buildings are privately occupied.

A business and shopping center extends from a point east of Nassau Street to the intersection of Boundary Street. It is not a part of the restored area, but the buildings have been designed in the style of the eighteenth century.

The College of William and Mary

A visitor who stands at the college gate, at the western end of Duke of Gloucester Street, and looks down the broad vista terminated in seven-eighths of a mile by the Capitol, will see at once the relationship of the College to the town plan of 1699. The orderly and symmetrical area of the college yard is also an architectural unit in itself. The central structure is the Wren Building, with its varying roof lines, massive chimneys, and lofty cupola. Flanking it at the north and south are the President's House and Brafferton Building, apparently identical in dimension and detail, although the Brafferton is actually somewhat smaller. These two buildings have narrow, many-paned windows and steep-pitched roofs, to give a strong balancing vertical accent to the architectural composition. On the central walk of the college yard stands the time-worn statue of Governor Botetourt, the work of the London sculptor Richard Hayward in 1773. Virginia's legislators commissioned this tribute to their beloved former governor, and for several years it had an honored place at the Capitol. It was knocked off its pedestal and suffered damage at the hands of misguided patriots during the Revolution, but was later repaired and in 1801 moved to its present position.

Wren Building. Restored. This is the oldest academic building in English-America. According to a contemporary it was "first modelled by Sir *Christopher Wren*," but "adapted to the Nature of the Country by the *Gentlemen* there." Originally known simply as "The College," it now bears the name of the distinguished English architect to whom it owes its general design. The cornerstone was laid in 1695, two years after the college had been chartered by King William and Queen Mary. Although serious damage was done by fire in 1705, 1859, and 1862, the exterior walls are largely original. The classrooms are in use today and they, together with the Blue Room on the second floor, the Great Hall, and the Chapel, have been restored to their early appearance.

The College of William and Mary was chartered in 1693 as an Anglican college "to the end that the Church of Virginia may be furnish'd with a Seminary of Ministers of the Gospel, and that the Youth may be piously educated in good Letters and Manners, and that the Christian Faith may be propagated amongst the Western Indians, to the Glory of Almighty God." Throughout the colonial period, William and Mary was the center of higher education in Virginia and Maryland, for both the tobacco colonies of the Chesapeake were taxed to support it. It is the second oldest college in the United States.

In the eighteenth century, long before Horace Mann and the great public-school movement, education was not easily come by in the colonies. There were a few endowed schools in Virginia, such as the Symmes-Eaton Academy of Elizabeth City County and "Matty Whaley's School" in Williamsburg; often a clergyman ran a small school, to serve his parish and augment his income; and the college itself had a grammar school. Sons of plantation owners, who commonly were entrusted to tutors at home for their schooling, could either attend William and Mary or go overseas to Oxford, Cambridge, or Edinburgh, or to read law at the Inns of Court in London. Higher education conferred considerable prestige on the few who attained it. Girls had little formal education.

Although the average enrollment at William and Mary was less than one hundred during the eighteenth century, the College exerted great influence on the intellectual life of Virginia and produced an extraordinary number of distinguished alumni, including Thomas Jefferson, James Monroe, and John Marshall. Four of the first ten presidents of the United States were associated with the College. George Washington for eleven years was chancellor. Edmund Randolph, attorney-general in Washington's cabinet, wrote: "Until the revolution, most of our leading [men] were the alumni of William and Mary."

The faculty included such distinguished men as the Reverend Hugh Jones, mathematician and grammarian, Dr. William Small, physicist, and George Wythe, jurist and classical teacher. "I know of no place in the world," wrote Jefferson in 1788, "while the present professors remain, where I would so soon place a son." In 1729 there were six professors in the three schools of Humanity, Philosophy, and Divinity. It was largely through the influence of alumnus Jefferson that the curriculum was broadened in 1780. Provision was made for chairs of Mathematics and Natural Philosophy, Law and Police, Chemistry and Medicine, Ethics and Belles Lettres, and Modern Languages. The chair of Divinity was discontinued. William and Mary had been founded as an Anglican college, but, as James Madison, President of the College explained, "it is now thought that Establishments in Favor of any particular Sect are incompatible with the Freedom of a Republic."

The visitor enters the Wren Building by the main (east) door flanked by two howitzers captured from Cornwallis at Yorktown. Passing through the central corridor he comes out on the "Piazza," overlooking the west courtyard and modern sunken garden. To the north is the Great Hall where faculty and students dined in common in the eighteenth century; it was here that the House of Burgesses met while awaiting the completion of the Capitol. At the south end of the piazza is the chapel wing, completed in 1732, where masters and students and an occasional distinguished visitor such as Lord Botetourt attended morning and evening prayers and special services. The fourth side of what was originally planned as a quadrangle was never added, although Jefferson drew plans for it about 1773. In the crypt of the Chapel are buried distinguished Virginians, including Sir John Randolph, Peyton Randolph, Bishop James Madison, and also the popular governor, Lord Botetourt. When the college is in session, guides are on hand to conduct visitors through the building.

President's House – N. Restored. Built in 1732-33 this house has been the residence of every president of the College of William and Mary. Its first occupant was the Reverend Dr. James Blair, the energetic Anglican clergyman from Scotland who first induced

the Virginia Assembly to favor the erection of a college and then, in 1693, persuaded King William and Queen Mary to charter and endow it. He also supervised the construction of all the early buildings and selected the first faculty and curriculum. Blair served as president for half a century. During the last stages of the Revolution, the house was used briefly as headquarters by Cornwallis, and after the Battle of Yorktown French officers serving under Lafayette and Rochambeau occupied it, causing accidental damage which Rochambeau at once ordered repaired at the expense of the French government. The eminent scientist James Madison lived here as President of the College (1777-1812). In 1790 he became the first Bishop of Virginia (previously a part of the Diocese of London).

The Brafferton Building – S. Restored. When Robert Boyle, the noted British scientist, died in 1691, he directed that the revenue from his estate Brafferton, in England, be devoted to charitable purposes. His executors later divided the fund between Harvard and William and Mary, where it was to be used to educate Indian youths. At first, Indians were quartered on the third floor of the Wren Building with masters and other students, but in 1723 this building was completed for their use. Until the Revolution cut off revenue from the Boyle foundation, there were always some—often a dozen or more— Indians at the College, although most seem to have forgotten their prayers and

catechism when they left Williamsburg. So far as is known, not one became a missionary as Boyle's executors had hoped. This building, which today provides offices and guest rooms for alumni, suffered remarkably little damage over the years.

Francis and France Streets
East to West

Benjamin Waller House–S. Restored. This L-shaped colonial house with gambrel-roofed wing was built soon after 1750 by Benjamin Waller, a prominent Williamsburg attorney. In an  impressive career, Waller held a variety of offices: he served as burgess, city recorder, judge of the Court of Admiralty, and vestryman of Bruton Parish. The property, which remained in his family for over a century, was subsequently owned and occupied by his great-grandson, William Waller, who married Elizabeth Tyler, the daughter of President John Tyler. Privately occupied.

Draper House–N. Reconstructed. This long, narrow, house-and-shop combination is admirably located on a corner of the Capitol Square. John Draper, a farrier  and smith who owned the property in the late eighteenth century, undoubtedly profited greatly because of his strategic site. Draper also kept a stable and during the Revolution helped to haul guns and general supplies for the "public service." Privately occupied.

Bassett Hall–S. Unrestored. This handsome, two-story building, to be seen from the entrance of the long driveway, is a good example of a small plantation house set off by outbuildings, gardens, and a fine, tree-shaded approach. It was erected about 1753 by Colonel Philip Johnson, a burgess who suffered financial reverses and soon afterward was forced to rent the house as a tavern. About 1800 the property was purchased by Colonel Burwell Bassett, Martha Washington's nephew. Among the galaxy of guests who visited the hospitable Colonel Bassett were Lafayette and the Irish poet Thomas Moore, who is said to have composed "To a Firefly" after watching lightning bugs in the gardens one summer evening. Privately occupied.

Carter-Moir House and Moir Shop-N. Reconstructed. In 1745 John Carter "obtain'd a License to retale Liquors," and advertised in the *Gazette* to give "Notice to all Persons who are desirous of cheap Entertainment, that they may be supply'd with good Pasture. . . . Also good lodging, either private or publick." By 1777 James Moir occupied the buildings on this property. A tailor by trade, he was also willing to accommodate students "to lodge, board, wash, and mend for them, at a very low price." Both buildings are privately occupied.

Ayscough House-N. Restored. At least one of the ways to Francis Fauquier's heart was through his stomach. When this popular governor died in 1768, he left a generous sum to Mrs. Christopher Ayscough in recognition of her able management of his kitchen. Probably it was with this bequest that she and her husband, who was Palace gardener, bought this lot and built their house. For a while the Ayscoughs operated a tavern, but in 1770 the house was rented and became a shop where the latest styles and trinkets from England could be displayed to catch the attention of those who flocked to Williamsburg in Public Times. Today a cabinetmaker plies his trade here in a craft shop open to the public.

Semple House-S. Restored. Unique in Williamsburg, this house is a harbinger of the Federal style of architecture which followed the Revolution. Although built prior to 1782, the classical

influence—soon to be felt throughout the young republic—is evident in the porch with its carefully modeled columns, elaborate cornice, and enriched pediment. The kitchen and covered passageway were later additions. The house was the home of James Semple, judge and law professor of the early 1800's. Privately occupied.

INTERSECTION OF BLAIR STREET

Robertson-Galt House–N. Unrestored. This house, recently acquired by Colonial Williamsburg and to be restored, was built sometime between 1707 and 1718 by William Robertson, for many years clerk of the Governor's Council. By 1749 it had become the property of William Nelson—a prominent political figure—in joint ownership with his even more distinguished son Thomas, a signer of the Declaration of Independence, commander of Virginia's forces in the Revolution, and third governor of the Commonwealth. It seems probable that Thomas Nelson lived here in the 1780's. Early in the next century the house came into the hands of the Galt family, notable citizens of Williamsburg from colonial days. Their descendants have lived here ever since. Privately occupied.

Chiswell-Bucktrout House–S. Restored. The roof line of this dwelling is unusual in Williamsburg though it was common in England at the beginning of the eighteenth century, the period when

the house was built. The form was established by a study of roof timbers and numbered beams in the surviving portions of the building. The owner, Colonel John Chiswell, was in 1766 the center of a controversy that "put the whole country into a ferment." Arrested for killing a Scottish merchant in a fit of rage, he was released on bail, an unusually lenient procedure which the less privileged attributed to his political and family connections. The Colonel died just before his trial—by his own hand, it was rumored. Benjamin Bucktrout, cabinetmaker and merchant, purchased the house in 1774. A guesthouse for Williamsburg Inn.

Providence Hall–S. This privately owned eighteenth-century house, standing well back from the street, was recently moved to Williamsburg from Providence Forge by its owner.

Ewing House–S. Restored. Ebenezer Ewing made his home here in the eighteenth century. He was one of the many Scotsmen who emigrated to colonial Virginia.

At his death in 1795 he left his property to his widow with the proviso that "the moment she marries . . . it becomes the property of my son . . . Thomas." Some years later, Thomas was bound out "to learn art of seaman or mariner," and either died or disappeared during his apprenticeship. The largest outbuilding to the house was a forge in early days. Privately occupied.

Intersection of Botetourt Street

Dr. Barraud House–N. Restored. An example of symmetry in colonial architecture, this comfortable dwelling was erected about 1780 and incorporates earlier buildings on the site. A massive gabled roof surmounts a typical Virginia house plan, with two rooms

on either side of a central hall. The light green of the cornice and porch is the original paint color found when the house was studied prior to restoration. The porch railing shows the Chinese influence prevalent in the second half of the eighteenth century. The early owner of the house was Dr. Philip Barraud, a public-spirited physician, active in the affairs of the College and of Eastern State Hospital. While on a visit to Norfolk in 1798, the doctor wrote a letter indicating his affection for his home; he asked his friend St. George Tucker to send him measurements of the "Sitting-Room Hearth" so that he might have a fender made "to protect us from Danger of burning the House & ravishing the lovely carpet." Barraud became superintendent of the Marine Hospital in Norfolk in 1799 and his house was sold in 1801 to Mrs. Anna Byrd, the widow of Otway Byrd. Privately occupied.

Moody House-S. Restored. This unpretentious house takes its name from Josiah Moody, who owned it from the 1790's until his death about 1810. Archaeological evidence indicates that it was built prior to 1750 and altered several times, reaching its present size and appearance by 1782. There is a long, lean-to roof on the south, usually an indication that additions were made to an earlier structure of smaller size. Privately occupied.

Powell-Hallam House-S. Restored. Sometime between 1753 and 1760, Benjamin Powell, a wheelwright and carpenter who rose to a position of prominence in Williamsburg, built a house on the York Road; later moved to this site, it will eventually be moved again. By local tradition it was in this house that Sarah Hallam lived after her retirement from the stage. Privately occupied.

Orrell House-S. Restored. In this, an otherwise typical gambrel-roof house, the entrance hall is not centered; all the living quarters are therefore to one side of the hall. The original house was probably built during the third quarter of the eighteenth century, and takes its name from John Orrell (often written Orrill) who owned it about 1800. A guesthouse for Williamsburg Inn.

Lewis House-N. Reconstructed. In recent years, before this house was reconstructed, its original chimney, standing alone in an otherwise vacant lot, was a familiar Williamsburg landmark. The site, originally part of the Orlando Jones property which extended from Duke of Gloucester Street to Francis Street, was separated soon after 1790 and came into the possession of one Charles Lewis, who owned it until 1806 and is believed to have built the house which stood here. A guesthouse for Williamsburg Inn.

INTERSECTION OF COLONIAL STREET

Williamsburg Inn–S. A modern hotel and restaurant, the Inn is owned and operated by Colonial Williamsburg. Designed after the manner of resort architecture of the early nineteenth century, it is particularly reminiscent of the Springs of Virginia, and contrasts with the colonial architecture of the restored area.

The Quarter–S. Restored. Little is known of this small, quaint, late eighteenth-century cottage, al-though it is believed to have served for a time as slave quarters to the adjoining property. The front por-tion of the house is typical of the 16-by-24-foot dwelling of the early 1700's. The addition of a shed por-tion at the rear has created an un-usual and attractive roof line. A guesthouse for Williamsburg Inn.

Bracken-Carter House–S. Reconstructed. This lot was part of a considerable amount of land in this section of Williamsburg owned by the Reverend John Bracken. It is marked on maps dating from the late eighteenth century as the property of "Js. Carter," and in 1804 Elizabeth Carter was living here. The architecture of the house is of the mid-1700's. A guesthouse for Williamsburg Inn.

Bracken House–S. Restored. Two large, T-shaped chimneys, characteristic of the early eighteenth century, lend weight to the

design of this typical Virginia house. The steep gabled roof is accented at the eaves by fine modillion cornices. The house is named for one of Wil-liamsburg's distinguished citizens, the Reverend John Bracken, who for many years owned it though there is no evidence that he lived here. Bracken became rector of Bruton Parish in 1773, soon after his arrival from England. He continued in that office for forty-five years, until his death, and in addition was mayor of Williamsburg in 1800. He was elected Bishop of Virginia in 1812 but declined consecration, presumably on account of his age and many local commitments, which included holding the presidency of the College from 1812 to 1814. Through his marriage in 1776 to Sally Burwell of Carter's Grove he was related to many leading families in Virginia and acquired considerable wealth. For many years he occupied, and ultimately bought, the Allen-Byrd House. Privately occupied.

Masonic Lodge–N. This modern building is privately owned, and was erected by the Williamsburg masons on the site of an eighteenth-century meeting place of this same Lodge. Established as early as 1751, local masons received

a new constitution and charter from England in 1773, in which year Peyton Randolph was elected Grand Master. Among early members were Edmund Randolph, President James Monroe, Bishop James Madison, St. George Tucker, and Peter Pelham.

Allen-Byrd House–S. Restored. Incorporating portions of an earlier house, this brick mansion was brought to its present appearance in 1769 by Colonel William Allen, a wealthy Surry County planter. It was purchased the following year by William Byrd III of Westover for a town house. A scion of one of the most famous families of colonial Virginia, Byrd served as a member of the House of Burgesses, and later on the Governor's Council. During the French and Indian War he raised and commanded the Second Virginia Regiment, paying all expenses out of his own pocket. Although a man of marked military talent, Byrd was deficient in business ability; he lived on a lavish scale and was overfond of gaming. It was rumored that he lost £10,000 to the Duke of Cumberland at a single sitting in a fashionable club in London's West End. He went through the accumulated wealth of his father and grandfather and was impoverished when he died in 1777. His plantation, Westover, passed out of the family and his own house was sold at auction before the door of Raleigh Tavern, together with the celebrated Byrd library "consisting of near 4000 volumes." The Allen-Byrd House was bought by the Reverend John Bracken who had for some time rented and occupied it. This fine residence, with brick walls laid in Flemish bond, is unusual in having a second floor as high as the first. The end walls are left blank to allow the fireplace side of each room to be free of windows, a practice not uncommon in the eighteenth century. The house is adorned by a robust belt course in molded brick and a wrought-iron balcony suggestive of the balcony at the Palace. The decorative front fence shows Chinese influence; at the back may be seen a wattled fence, made of vines. The outbuildings, some of a distinctive dusky red color, have been reconstructed on colonial foundations. Privately occupied.

Intersection of South England Street

Roscow Cole's Office–S. Reconstructed. This small, clapboard building now houses the Williamsburg Public Library. The site is part of the property on which the James City County Courthouse was built in 1715. Roscow Cole owned it from 1819 to 1835, and used a small building which stood here as an office.

Roscow Cole's Laundry–S. Reconstructed. The original of this typical small building was described in an insurance policy of 1801, at which time it was valued at $100. Old photographs further assisted the architects in the reconstruction. Used first as a kitchen, then as a laundry, it is now a private law office.

Market Square Pump–N. Reconstructed. The well, foundations of which were discovered at this location on the edge of Market Square, is thought to have been established under a statute of 1762. In order "to supply water for the fire engine," the City of Williamsburg was authorized to levy a tax to defray the expense of "sinking wells . . . and fixing pumps therein," a measure which it was hoped would "conduce to the preservation of the said city." The well-house is conjectural, the design based on English precedents of the period.

Custis Kitchen–S. From the street it is possible to catch a glimpse of a small brick building, standing alone in the eastern portion of the grounds of Eastern State Hospital. Known locally as Martha Washington's Kitchen, it is all that remains of the Custis estate. About 1715 Colonel John Custis — scholar, planter, and eccentric — acquired the property, subsequently known as Custis Square, and built a brick residence on it. Here Custis lived and cultivated his celebrated garden, vestiges of which still remained at the time of the Civil War. On his death in 1749, the property passed to his son, Daniel Parke Custis, who lived here with his wife until his own death in 1757. The widow Custis subsequently married George Washington. Washington administered the property until his stepson, John Parke Custis, came of age in 1778, at which time Custis Square was sold at auction. In 1843, it was acquired by Eastern State Hospital.

Eastern State Hospital–S. Founded in 1770, and long known as the "Lunatick Hospital," this is one of the earliest state-owned hospitals in America devoted entirely to mental illness. In colonial times the care of the insane, like the care of paupers, was considered a local matter and usually was left to the vestry of the parish. The vestry was unable to finance or maintain an asylum, and hence the insane were either left at large in a world with which they could not cope or placed in prison where they were often badly mistreated. The humane Governor Francis Fauquier, realizing this, directed the attention of the burgesses to the need for better care for "persons who are so unhappy as to be deprived of their reason," and an act was passed in 1770 "to make Provision for the support and maintenance of ideots, lunatics, and other persons of unsound Minds." The Hospital, designed by a well-known Philadelphia architect, Robert Smith, was opened in 1773. Among its original trustees were Peyton Randolph, George Wythe, Thomas Nelson "The Signer," John Blair, John Tazewell, and John Randolph "The Tory." Disastrous fires in 1876 and 1885 razed all principal colonial buildings. Today the hospital has about 1800 patients and a staff of 250.

Griffin House–S. Unrestored. Built sometime prior to 1782, this house was owned by Samuel Griffin, a Revolutionary officer who became a member of the Continental Congress. Griffin married the daughter of Carter Braxton, one of the Virginia signers of the Declaration of Independence. Privately occupied.

Nicholson Street—East to West

Coke-Garrett House–N. Restored. After being owned successively by a baker, an ordinary keeper, a barber, a "Gentleman," a gaoler, a joiner, a perukemaker, and a carpenter, this house and lot came into the possession of John Coke about 1755. Coke, a successful goldsmith and tavern keeper, left an estate valued at £772 when he died in the mid-1760's. His widow, Sarah, continued to operate the house as a tavern. In 1777 she was forced to petition the House of Delegates to compensate her for damage done by Continental troops quartered here. The property was acquired by the Garrett family of Williamsburg about 1813 and remained in its

possession for well over a century. The house is actually two separate dwellings, joined end to end, with a detached office near by. The small hooded west porch supported by columns is a typical Virginia porch of the period. The fine garden, often mentioned in court records, forms part of a plantation layout in miniature; a flanking garden to the east has yet to be restored. The garden is largely evergreen, the various sections separated by hedges of ancient dwarf box. In the lower parterre, bulbs and annuals are planted in the pie-shaped beds produced by the so-called British flag design. The small family graveyard at the rear was a common feature in colonial Virginia. The house is privately occupied; the garden, open to the public, is entered through a gate near the Gaol.

The Public Gaol

On the northern side of Nicholson Street stands the Public Gaol, referred to by a reliable eighteenth-century chronicler as a "strong sweet Prison." After 250 years it remains today grim evidence of crime and punishment in colonial America. Now restored, it is an Exhibition Building of Colonial Williamsburg. Both common criminals awaiting summary justice and debtors awaiting succor or mercy were confined here. The imprisonment of debtors, however, was practically eliminated after 1772 as the result of an act making creditors wholly responsible for the maintenance of debtors and trebling the fees for their board. The General Court, which met twice a year at the Capitol, tried criminals punishable by mutilation or death. Under certain circumstances civil suits involving claims in excess of £10 sterling or 2,000 pounds of tobacco were also heard. Lesser criminals were forced to undergo the discomfort and public ridicule of the pillory or stocks, barbarous but effective instruments of justice which today's visitors may try out without the inconvenience of a padlock.

Henry Cary, the master builder who supervised construction of both Capitol and Palace, was ordered by the Assembly to begin work in 1701 on a "Publick Gaol" (pronounced "jail" as today). By 1704, the Gaol was ready to receive its first guests. Debtors' cells were added in 1711. Keeper's quarters were built in 1722, the period to which the building has been restored. The Gaol served colony and commonwealth until 1780, and thereafter a portion of the original building continued to be used by Williamsburg and James City County until 1933, when it was deeded by the city to Colonial Williamsburg. Part of the brickwork of its massive walls is original and some of the early interior finish was found. In the course of excavations, shackles were unearthed, evidence of the bleak life of an unlucky few.

Though frequently tempered with mercy, the treatment and disposition of criminals in the Virginia Colony seems inhumane in the light of prison reforms of the past two centuries. Yet it should be recalled that colonial society included not only the usual lawless elements but newly arrived slaves, transported convicts, runaway indentured servants, pirates, and marauding Indians. It was a society not far removed from the frontier and one in which hot tempers, high spirits, and little education often produced crimes of the worst sort. Furthermore, it was costly to build and maintain prisons; it was customary to clear criminal cells of their inmates after each session of the General Court. Thus, with the exception of debtors, persons convicted by this Court were usually fined, lashed, branded, mutilated, or hanged. Debtors who could not gain relief through friends or family were forced to await the ultimate mercy of the Court.

Yet despite leg irons, handcuffs, and chains, despite bitter cold nights spent on floor matting of malodorous straw, and despite a diet of "salt beef damaged, and Indian meal," the life of the prisoners was not wholly without mitigation. During daylight hours they were often allowed to walk about and converse in the exercise yard. Sanitary arrangements, though crude, were advanced for that century. In cases of illness, "Physick" was provided, and more fortunate prisoners were permitted to return to their homes until recovery. Those with an adequate purse could buy meals or liquor from one of the taverns in the vicinity, and often shared these luxuries with others. A group of Indians, thrown into the unheated cells in the winter of 1704-5, was provided with greatcoats by the Assembly. One keeper, in advertising the detention of a runaway slave, urged his owner to "make as speedy application for him as possible that he may not suffer from the inclemency of the season."

A prisoner sentenced to death was allowed several weeks to make his peace with God, and during this period was brought each Sunday to Bruton Parish Church by the gaoler. The death penalty was inflicted for many offenses, including arson, piracy, horse stealing, forgery, and burglary. Cases were carefully weighed, however, and clemency sometimes offered first offenders or criminals with a particularly moving plea. In 1718 thirteen henchmen of the notorious pirate Blackbeard were imprisoned in the Gaol, and eleven of them subsequently hanged; yet in 1727, John Vidal, a convicted pirate who pitifully protested that he "never intended to go a-pirating" and who "with a weeping heart" prayed for a longer time for repentance, was granted his Majesty's most gracious pardon.

The Gaol also served at times as a madhouse and military prison. The mentally ill were often confined here until the erection of Eastern State Hospital. During the turbulent early years of the Revolution, the Gaol was badly overcrowded with British redcoats, Tory sympathizers, traitors, deserters, and spies. Gaol fever broke out among them and many died, although the fever was controlled somewhat by cleaning the vaults and washing the floors with vinegar and sprinkling them with wild mint. The most famous prisoner during this period was General Henry Hamilton, the British Governor of the Northwest Territory, widely known as the "Hair Buyer" because he was believed to pay his Indian allies for American scalps.

The keeper's quarters are furnished with simple, serviceable pieces. Gaol keepers were paid little, and had a rough and dangerous job. The first keeper, John Redwood, received only thirty pounds annually. Each of his twelve colonial successors, despite increased pay, complained that his income was inadequate to the hazards of the office. One gaoler, "knock'd down" by a quart bottle in the hand of an escaping murderer, was discharged for his pains. The best-known keeper was the erudite Peter Pelham, who augmented his income by playing the organ at Bruton Parish Church, providing music for the second theatre, and teaching young ladies to master the harpsichord and spinnet. Pelham was musical director when *The Beggar's Opera* was first performed in Williamsburg. There were some who suggested that Pelham further increased his income by permitting convicted prisoners to escape, but he was cleared of all charges against him in an inquiry ordered by the Assembly.

INTERSECTIONS OF
BOTETOURT, COLONIAL, AND QUEEN STREETS

Tayloe House – N. Restored. Built early in the eighteenth century, this gambrel-roofed dwelling changed hands in 1759 for £600—a very high price for a frame house at that time. It was purchased as a town house by one of the wealthiest of colonial Virginians, Colonel John Tayloe, owner of the magnificent plantation Mount Airy on the Northern Neck. Tayloe served as justice as soon as he came of age, and was later for many years a member of the Governor's Council. Although a firm supporter of the rights of the colonies and a warm friend of Washington, Tayloe could not  reconcile himself to complete separation from Great Britain, and declined to serve when elected a member of the new commonwealth's council in 1776. The office, just east of the house, has an interesting ogee (S-shaped) roof. Terraced gardens once stretched down the gentle slope at the rear of the house. Privately occupied.

Peyton Randolph House – N. Restored. Here lived Peyton Randolph, one of the leading statesmen of colonial America. Randolph, who was speaker of the House of Burgesses from 1766 until 1775, was known as a conservative, but supported the colonies in their struggle with Great Britain and was president of the First

Continental Congress in Philadelphia in 1774. The house was erected sometime prior to 1723, when it was acquired by Sir John Randolph who left it to his son Peyton at his death in 1737. Peyton Randolph lived in it until his own death in 1775. During the Revolution, Rochambeau set up headquarters here prior to the Yorktown campaign, at the same time that Washington occupied the George Wythe House. The property was owned by the Peachy family in the nineteenth century and Mrs. Mary Monroe Peachy entertained Lafayette here on his visit to Williamsburg in 1824. The western portion, which was built first, was square with a large central chimney serving corner fireplaces. The eastern wing, with dormers, was built next, and the house took its present shape when the two were linked together. Noteworthy features are the wooden belt course at the second-floor line, the two-story porch chamber on the northern façade reminiscent of seventeenth-century architecture, and the hooded front entrance. Inside the house are outstanding panelings of pine, quartered oak, and polished walnut. Privately occupied.

INTERSECTION OF NORTH ENGLAND STREET

Archibald Blair House–N. Restored. This property was acquired in 1716 by Dr. Archibald Blair, and the frame house, a full two stories with no dormers in the roof, was erected soon afterward. On each floor, there are two rooms on either side of a central hall,

each room with a generous corner fireplace. Although the front porch is later in date than the house, it was retained because of its architectural appeal. Dr. Blair was a Scottish physician who emigrated to Virginia in 1690, perhaps because of the position and influence of his brother, the Reverend James Blair, subsequently founder and first president of the College of William and Mary. Archibald Blair supplemented the practice of medicine with the pursuits of commerce and conducted a business described by Governor Spotswood in 1718 as "one of the most considerable Trading Stores in this Country." Blair was for many years a vestryman of Bruton Church and a burgess for Jamestown. Blair died in 1735, and the house later became the property of John Randolph "The Tory," who sold it to Dr. Peter Hay in 1763. Eight years later it was recovered by Archibald's son John, and eventually passed to his son, Dr. James Blair, a physician. During the Revolution it was occupied briefly by James Madison, President of the College of William and Mary and later first Bishop of Virginia. Privately occupied.

St. George Tucker House—N. Restored. One of Williamsburg's most admired houses, this residence is marked by its repeating gabled roofs of various sizes, its widely spaced dormer windows, and its massive chimneys. Because of its narrow width, the second story has excellent light and ventilation, but requires five stairways. The earliest owner of the house was the noted jurist St. George Tucker, and it has continued in the possession of his family ever

since. Tucker, who became known as the "American Blackstone" because of his annotated edition of the celebrated *Commentaries,* published in 1803, purchased the property in 1788. He moved to this site an older building—believed to be the Levingston House—and enlarged it by several additions. Tucker, a native of Bermuda, attended the College of William and Mary and was active in the cause of the colonies during the Revolution. He was appointed judge of the Virginia General Court in 1788, and Federal district judge in 1813; in 1790 he succeeded George Wythe as professor of law at the College. His stepson was John Randolph of Roanoke. Tucker had two sons of his own, Nathaniel Beverley and Henry St. George. The former, who lived in the house from 1837 to 1851, was an ardent defender of the cause of the South and author of two controversial books, *The Partisan Leader* and *George Balcombe.* Privately occupied.

Palace Green—East Side

Levingston Kitchen–E. Reconstructed. The original building on this site was a dependency of the house of William Levingston, who built his theatre on the adjacent lot. The smaller building remained for some time after the house itself had been removed, possibly to become part of the St. George Tucker House. The massive chimney and the heavy cornice overhang, which provides added room on the second floor, give the kitchen architectural distinction. Privately occupied.

Site of the First Theatre in English America–E. Archaeologists unearthed here the foundations of the first theatre in America. Research has not yet revealed enough information about its appearance to warrant reconstruction. Foundations prove the building to have been only 30 feet wide by 80 feet long. This is not, however, conspicuously small in comparison with English provincial theatres of the period. William Levingston, a merchant from New Kent County, moved to Williamsburg early in the eighteenth century and erected the theatre about 1716. The lot was granted to him by enthusiastic trustees of the city for a yearly rent of "one grain of Indian corn." In *The Present State of Virginia,* published in England in 1724, the Reverend Hugh Jones referred to it as "a Play House and a good Bowling Green." In spite of his auspicious start impressario Levingston suffered financial reverses and was forced in 1721 to mortgage the property, and in 1727 to sell the theatre and leave Williamsburg. However, the building continued to be used periodically; in the autumn of 1736, *The Tragedy of Cato, The Busy-Body, The Recruiting Officer,* and *The Beaux' Stratagem* were performed here by "the young Gentlemen of the College." In later years, playgoers attended the city's second theatre near the Capitol. In 1745 the old playhouse was purchased for £50 by a group of subscribers and given to the City of Williamsburg to be used as a municipal court and city hall. It was repaired and reshingled and served as a Hustings Court until 1770, when it was apparently razed.

Brush-Everard House

The most recently restored Exhibition Building of Colonial Williamsburg is the Brush-Everard House on the east side of Palace Green. This frame building, long known to readers of Mary Johnstone's popular novel *Audrey* as the home of the heroine, was built in 1717 by John Brush, gunsmith, armorer, and first keeper of the colony's magazine on Market Square. Apparently the building served him both as shop and residence. William Dering, teacher of dancing at the College, bought the property in 1742. His importance in the social life of Williamsburg is indicated by an advertisement in the *Virginia Gazette* of September 11, 1746, announcing that "for the Entertainment of Gentlemen and Ladies, there will be Balls and Assemblies at the Capitol, every other Night, during the Court, by their humble Servant, William Dering." An unusually large number of pictures and "one paint box" in the inventory of Dering's estate have given rise to the belief that he was also an artist.

The house came eventually into the hands of Thomas Everard, who was clerk of York County from 1745 until his death in 1784. He served also as Auditor of Virginia and Clerk of the General Court. In 1766 he was elected mayor of Williamsburg and undoubtedly lived in the city at that time. A man of comfortable circumstances, though not wealthy, Everard is believed to have enlarged the house and embellished the interior. The addition of two wings at the rear resulted in a U-shaped plan, of which Williamsburg has one other example in the Elkanah Deane House. The staircase in the house is remarkably fine, with elaborately turned balusters and sweeping hand rails. The step brackets are richly ornamented with original carving almost identical in design and execution to the famous staircases at Carter's Grove in James City County, and Tuckahoe in Goochland County. The first-floor front rooms and central hall have paneled wainscoting. In two other rooms there is wallpaper which reproduces the design of fragments found in the house.

The yard between the house and the outbuildings is paved with the original brick disclosed in the course of excavations. Four turf panels run back to the lot line as it existed when Brush owned the property. Later the garden was enlarged and a small pond added— an unusual feature in colonial Williamsburg. Today the ancient box claims first attention. Dwarf box, originally forming a hedge on each side of the axial garden walk, has grown in a hundred and fifty years into a mass of tall twisted trees, the oldest box in Williamsburg.

Everard was a gentleman of standing in the community, though less celebrated than George Wythe and other prominent Virginians who were his friends. The Brush-Everard House represents a town house somewhat more modest than the Wythe House near by, and the furnishings have been chosen accordingly. It is a more difficult matter to depict the furnishing of a man's mind, but a library has been assembled in the house based upon a list compiled by Thomas Jefferson in 1771 for the guidance of a well-to-do planter of average intellectual interests.

Consisting of about 300 volumes, this library shows in tangible form an important element in the cultural life of colonial Virginia. The titles are distributed among the classics, drama, history, law, philosophy, religion, and science. In a letter explaining his selection, Jefferson rejected the notion that "nothing can be useful but the learned lumber of Greek and Roman reading," and maintained that "a little attention . . . to the nature of the human mind evinces that the entertainments of fiction are useful as well as pleasant." Jefferson calculated the cost of this library at about £100 sterling in plain bindings, and half as much again in fine marbled bindings.

The Governor's Palace

Reconstructed on its old foundations, the Palace—symbol of the power and prestige of the Crown in colonial Virginia—stands once more in a commanding position at the northern end of Palace Green. It is an Exhibition Building of Colonial Williamsburg. This was the official residence of seven royal governors, from Alexander Spotswood, who supervised its building, to the Earl of Dunmore, who fled from it at dawn one June morning in 1775, thus ending for all time British rule in Virginia. When the new commonwealth came into being, the Palace served as the executive mansion for the first two governors, Patrick Henry and Thomas Jefferson.

In 1706, a few years after the capital of the colony had been moved to Williamsburg from Jamestown, the Assembly was prevailed upon to set aside three thousand pounds for the erection of an official mansion for the governors. Henry Cary, the "master builder" who supervised the construction of the Capitol, was given charge and Alexander Spotswood, governor from 1710 to 1722, devoted his personal attention to the project. The building was not formally completed until about 1720, by which time it had earned the derisive sobriquet of "Palace" from colonists who resented the additional levies which had been required for its construction. In 1724, the Reverend Hugh Jones described it as "a magnificent Structure . . . finished and beautified with Gates, fine Gardens, Offices, Walks, a fine Canal, Orchards, &c."

The Palace, including the composition of buildings which surrounds it, is admirably adapted to express its dual function as a residence and as the official headquarters of the king's deputy in a great agricultural colony. The main building is usually described as Georgian in style, and in many respects resembles English country estates of the period of the first two Georges. The official character of the Palace is suggested in the playfully fortified effect created by the castellated walls in the forecourt, and is emphasized in the stately cupola (or lantern) rising above the balustraded roof. For special occasions the lantern was brilliantly illuminated. Dutch influence, introduced into England by William III, is discernible in this, and in other features. The Renaissance is reflected in the formal gardens and the orderly layout of the flanking buildings and other dependencies—which originally included stables. But the broad chimneys of the outbuildings and the characteristic shapes of smokehouse, laundry, wellhead, and salthouse lend a distinctly Virginia flavor, suggesting a plantation on the outskirts of town. In its unification of many converging influences, the Palace bears the unmistakable stamp of Virginia plantation architecture; it could have been built only in the colonial South.

In 1751 extensive repair work was authorized and the interior is believed to have been remodeled. It was probably at this time that a wing was added to provide a ballroom and supper room adequate for the official entertaining required of the royal representative. An invitation to the Palace was a distinction and might well serve a political purpose as well as the personal pleasure of the governor and his lady. In 1769 Lord Botetourt mentioned in a letter, "Fifty two dined with me yesterday, and I expect at least that number today." To the formal dining room, food was carried in great covered containers from the service area west of the building. Of course entertainment was costly; Governor Gooch ruefully noted that a celebration at a royal "Birth-Night" drew 100 guineas from his own purse. Along with the expense of servants and food, the "Binn Cellar," with hundreds of gallons of imported wines, had to be replenished.

The Upper Middle Room recalls the more intimate side of Palace life. Here the governor could be at ease with a few friends—perhaps enjoying a hot drink seasoned with spices from a rosewood box like the one now standing on the center table—or could peruse the latest volume to arrive from England. After long search, appropriate editions of all the books listed in Governor Botetourt's library have been assembled in this pleasant room. Other rooms tell other stories: in the east flanking building is the governor's office, with its Chinese Chippendale chest and gilt birdcage; the opposite flanking building, furnished as a guardhouse, serves as a reminder that Lord Dunmore once felt it necessary to station marines at the Palace for his protection—a precaution which would not have been dreamed of by such popular predecessors as Governors Fauquier and Botetourt.

In the gardens, yet another story was revealed: in the course of excavations for the reconstruction, twentieth-century investigators found tragic evidence of patriot troops who died while the Palace was serving as a military hospital during the Yorktown campaign. In eleven orderly rows were discovered the unmarked graves of 156 Revolutionary veterans and two women thought to have been nurses. Today a simple stone tablet commemorates their sacrifice and the branches of a weeping willow shade the plot.

At the Palace, as in the less pretentious gardens of Williamsburg, the formality of English design is seen. Here we find elaborate geometrical parterres, framed with clipped hedges, and accented with topiary work. Pleached alleys offer shade, and the plain parterre of the tree-box garden affords a green for a game of bowls. Standing watch over the garden are twelve massive box trees, the "twelve apostles" often found on English estates of the period. Additional "deceits" were added for the pleasure of the governor and his friends. One such is the holly maze, patterned after the maze at Hampton Court; it is overlooked by a lofty, tree-shaded mount built above a colonial icehouse. The canal and terraced gardens to the west of the Palace were apparently controversial features to budget-minded legislators, for Governor Spotswood in 1718 offered "if the Assembly did not care to be at the Expence of the Fish-Pond & Falling Gardens, to take them to my Self."

The colony provided "standing furniture" for the Palace but most of the furnishings were the personal property of the governor, imported by him from England or purchased from his predecessor.

When a governor died in Virginia, a careful accounting was rendered, and it has been from these inventories that the reconstructed building has been furnished. Virtually all furnishings of the Palace are antiques, acquired for the most part in England.

Excavations at the Palace site disclosed that the original basement walls were largely intact, and also revealed the foundations of most dependencies. Research workers were aided by a floor plan of the main building drawn by Thomas Jefferson in 1779 during his term as Governor of the Commonwealth, and also by a copperplate discovered in the Bodleian Library at Oxford; this engraving shows the front elevation of the Palace in considerable detail. The so-called Frenchman's Map of 1782, the work of an unknown French cartographer, offered additional evidence of the general layout of the buildings and grounds. Further significant information was contained in the journals of the House of Burgesses and in other colonial records. Reconstruction, begun in 1930, necessitated provision for a new building elsewhere to house Matthew Whaley School which occupied the Palace site.

Palace Green—West Side

Carter-Saunders House–W. Restored. This stately old house was built sometime prior to 1746. For a time in 1751, while the Palace was undergoing repairs, it served as the residence of Governor Dinwiddie. The first known owner was Charles Carter, son of Robert "King" Carter. He sold the property in 1746, but in 1752 it was purchased by another member of the family, Robert Carter Nicholas, long a leader of the conservative faction of the house of Burgesses and Treasurer of the Colony. Nicholas made it his home until  1761, when he sold it to his cousin, Councilor Robert Carter of Nomini Hall. Carter was a true product of the eighteenth-century enlightenment—a cultivated gentleman, a liberal, and a patriot.

He lived in the house for twelve years and here entertained many distinguished persons including, on more than one occasion, George Washington. Of the seventeen Carter children, six were born here. In 1773 Carter wrote Peyton Randolph that he and Mrs. Carter considered their Williamsburg house "not sufficiently roomy" for their family. They accordingly withdrew to their country estate, Nomini Hall, on the Northern Neck. Philip Fithian, tutor to the children, left in his journal and letters a valuable account of plantation life. In 1801 the Williamsburg property was sold to Robert Saunders who bequeathed it to his son Robert, fourteenth president of the College. The linking of outbuildings with the main house by means of extended covered ways gives an impression of the scale of domestic operations in a gentleman's household. The brick outbuilding is original; other dependencies were reconstructed on old foundations from numerous documentary records.

Elkanah Deane House–W. Reconstructed. The original dwelling on this site was purchased by Elkanah Deane, an Irish coachmaker, who, in 1772, paid £700 for the house, shop, and garden—sufficient evidence of the prosperity of one of Williamsburg's successful craftsmen.

Deane may have been encouraged to move to Williamsburg because while working in New York he was ordered to make a coach, phaeton, and chaise for Governor Dunmore. Although described by one disgruntled rival in the *Gazette* as "an Hibernian Cottager" and the "Palace Street Puffer," Deane earned a name for himself making and repairing all kinds of carriages, harness, steel springs, and ironwork, as well as painting, gilding, and japanning. He died in 1775. The house itself disappeared soon after 1800. The plan resembles that of the Brush-Everard House, the U in this case enclosing a back porch which looks out over a formal garden. The tree-box topiary and overhead clipped canopy of American sweet gums are conspicuous features. Privately occupied.

INTERSECTION OF PRINCE GEORGE STREET

George Wythe House

In this solid brick mansion on the west side of Palace Green, now restored as one of the Exhibition Buildings of Colonial Williamsburg, lived George Wythe, a mild-mannered, soft-spoken man who was one of the most influential Americans of his era. Wythe (pronounced to rhyme with Smith) was a product of Virginia's plantation society. He was born in 1726 in Elizabeth City County where his father, who died soon after, was a successful planter. Wythe attended school at William and Mary for a brief time and encouraged by his mother, read widely in the classics, a custom frequently followed by cultured members of the gentry. He became perhaps the foremost classical scholar in Virginia. After studying law for a short time, he was admitted to the bar at the age of twenty. For a few years he practiced law in Spotsylvania, in partnership with John Lewis. In 1747 he married Lewis' sister Ann, who unfortunately died within a year of the ceremony.

Williamsburg became Wythe's home about 1754, when he was

elected to represent the city as a burgess. At this time he also acted
as the colony's attorney-general while his friend Peyton Randolph
was on a mission in England. It was also about this time that he
married Elizabeth Taliaferro (pronounced Tolliver), daughter of
Colonel Richard Taliaferro, who is believed to have designed and
built the Wythe House for his daughter and son-in-law. Their only
child died in infancy.

The public career of George Wythe spanned a decisive half-
century in American life: as executor and close friend of the popular
royal governors Fauquier and Botetourt, he saw the power of the
Crown at its height; as a burgess during most of the years from the
mid-century to the Revolution (and clerk of the House from 1769
to 1775), he sided with the patriots in the growing dispute with
Parliament; as a legislator and justice during the formation of the
young republic, he fought for independence, the protection of individual liberties, and the authority of the courts. He ably supported
Richard Henry Lee's resolution for independence at Philadelphia,
and his name appears first among Virginia signers of the Declaration
of Independence. He counseled Virginia to establish a regular army
instead of a militia, and himself volunteered for service, but he was
chosen instead to become Speaker of the House of Delegates in 1777,
and in 1778, one of the three judges of Virginia's High Court of
Chancery. Working with Jefferson and Edmund Pendleton, he aided
in revising the laws of Virginia.

This distinguished record was, however, fully matched in importance by Wythe's influence as a teacher and adviser. He probably
did more to shape Jefferson's ideas than any other man. Wythe first
knew the future President as a thoughtful, freckle-faced student at
the College of William and Mary. Later Jefferson studied law in
Wythe's office, and referred to him as "my faithful and beloved
Mentor in youth, and my most affectionate friend through life."
The Jefferson family stayed at the Wythe House for several weeks
in 1776.

In 1779, Wythe was appointed to the newly established chair of
law at William and Mary, and thus became the first professor of
law in an American college. Among his students was John Marshall,
Chief Justice of the United States Supreme Court. Henry Clay was
later his amanuensis. Wythe's brilliant career ended tragically in
1806 when he was poisoned, probably by George Sweeney a grand-

nephew who hoped to profit as the principal beneficiary under his uncle's will. Sweeney, grandson of Wythe's only sister, was in desperate financial straits. He is alleged to have poured arsenic into coffee, causing the death also of a servant. The aged statesman lived in agony for a week, long enough to disinherit his nephew. Sweeney was never convicted, however, largely because the testimony of a slave who witnessed the act was not then admissible in Virginia courts. Like many Virginians of his time, Wythe opposed slavery in principle and freed his servants in his will. To Jefferson—then president — he bequeathed his "books and small philosophical apparatus," and his "silver cups and goldheaded cane." He is buried in St. John's Churchyard, Richmond.

The Wythe House served as headquarters for Washington just prior to the siege of Yorktown, and for Rochambeau after the surrender of Cornwallis. It passed through the hands of many owners, and in 1926 was purchased by interested individuals and organizations and given to Bruton Church to be used as a parish house. Some restoration work was undertaken at that time. In 1938, after it was acquired by Colonial Williamsburg, restoration of the building and grounds was completed.

House, outbuildings, and gardens form a plantation layout in miniature. A large vegetable garden provided produce for the family table and fowls were kept in the chicken house. Other provisions brought from the country were stored in the smokehouse and elsewhere. The mansion, typical in plan, is spacious but simple. Two rooms on each side flank the large central hall on both the first and second story. Two great chimneys rise between the paired rooms, thus affording a fireplace in all eight. The smaller windows in the second story have the same number of panes as those on the first floor, a device which adds to the apparent scale of the house. Horizontal brick lines at the water table and at the belt course between the first and second floors relieve the severe lines of the exterior. Furnishings include both English and American pieces, predominantly those of the late eighteenth century. No inventory has been discovered, although a few orders sent by Wythe to England were found; the house, therefore, has been refurnished with the guidance of inventories of similar houses, owned by men of similar wealth and background.

The garden is enclosed on two sides by the main house and out-

buildings, which form an L along Palace Green and Prince George
Street. Behind the house extends a pleasure garden, lined with tree-
box topiary and terminated in a pleached arbor of hornbeam. Brick
and marl paths link the service area, kitchen garden, and herb garden
with the main house.

The Wythe House South Office-W. Reconstructed. Here, in
a craft shop open to the public, spinning and weaving are carried on
by the methods used in colonial times when the duties of the
housewife included making fabrics for her household.

Prince George Street—East to West

Deane Shop and Forge-N. Reconstructed. Once the workshop of coachmaker Elkanah Deane, this is now a craft shop open
to the public. Here a blacksmith—one who works in that "black
metal" iron—fashions and repairs all kinds of ironware using the
simple tools of the eighteenth century. The iron is thrust into a

forge kept glowing by means of
a hand-operated bellows, then
shaped and welded with hammer
and chisel on an ancient anvil.
Outside the shop a horse's head,
handsomely painted, announces
the blacksmith's trade. In Williamsburg the shoeing of horses
was a small part of the black-
smith's work. The soil in the Tidewater being sandy and free of
stones, horses for the most part were unshod in colonial times. Every
farm and every home needed some items of the hardware the smith
produced, whether wagon wheels or smoothing irons. Like other
skilled craftsmen, he was well paid for his labor, and he was often
a man of substantial wealth and social standing.

Matthew Whaley School. Looking north at the intersection of
Nassau Street a modern building can be seen which houses one of
Williamsburg's oldest institutions. The Matthew Whaley School, a
public elementary and high school, is named in memory of a nine-
year-old boy who died in 1705. His widowed mother bequeathed
more than £500 to "eternalize" her son through a "free school."

Timson House. On the northwest corner of Prince George and Nassau streets is one of the oldest houses in Williamsburg, built prior to 1717. It is privately owned and has not been restored.

South England Street—South to North

Tazewell Hall-W. In colonial days this house was the central portion of a plantation mansion which had two flanking wings and was surrounded by outbuildings. Behind it stretched ninety acres of tobacco fields and woodland. Sir John Randolph, who lived here, was knighted by King George II for his services to the colony and the Crown—the only native-born Virginian to be so honored. Peyton Randolph, his son, deeded the property to his brother John, "The Tory," one of the few members of Virginia's planter aristocracy who went to England to live rather than abandon loyalty to the Crown. He was the last attorney general of the Virginia colony; his son Edmund Randolph—born in this house—served in Washington's cabinet as the first attorney general of the new republic. In 1775 the Hall was sold to John Tazewell. It was moved to its present location when the city extended South England Street.

Williamsburg Lodge-W. A modern hotel with public restaurants, owned and operated by Colonial Williamsburg.

Reception Center-E. A temporary building houses the Information Office and Reception Center of Colonial Williamsburg, where a brief program of motion pictures and color slides is offered as an introduction to Virginia's early capital. In the evenings plays, illustrated lectures, and other special events are scheduled. Tickets to the Exhibition Buildings are on sale as well as official publications, post cards, and color slides. Public rest rooms are provided. There is no charge for admission to the interpretation program.

Craft House-E. Reproductions of the furniture and furnishings in the Exhibition Buildings of Colonial Williamsburg are displayed, and may be purchased, at the Craft House. These reproductions, including silver, furniture, glass, china, brass, pewter, iron, fabrics, paint, wallpaper, prints, and needlework, have been developed under the Reproduction Program of Williamsburg Restoration, Incorporated. Books and articles reminiscent of eighteenth-century Williamsburg are also available here. A Travel Office is located in the lobby for the convenience of visitors.

Courthouse for James City County and the City of Williamsburg – W. Although designed in the manner of the eighteenth century, this is a modern building, serving as courthouse for the City of Williamsburg and James City County. It is appropriately situated, because in 1715 a small courthouse for the county was erected somewhere on this same plot. In 1770 a new courthouse—still standing on Duke of Gloucester Street—was built to house the County Court and also the municipal court which had for some years occupied the theatre building on Palace Green. The property on Francis Street was then acquired by Robert Carter Nicholas, treasurer of the colony and later a Chancery Court judge. Nicholas built a large frame house here and numerous outbuildings. Among the subsequent owners was John Tyler, tenth President of the United States. Tyler, as the newly elected vice-president, was living here in 1841 when word reached Williamsburg that President William Henry Harrison had died. The new President is said to have been playing marbles in his yard with several small boys when he heard the news—a delightful, if apocryphal, legend.

Waller Street—South to North

Site of Second Williamsburg Theatre – E. Soon after the discontinuance of the First Theatre a movement was begun to erect a new "Play House" near the Capitol, and subscriptions for this purpose were encouraged by the visit to America of the famous English "Company of Commedians," headed by Walter Murray and Thomas Kean. On October 21, 1751, the new theatre, complete with pit, boxes, and gallery, opened with their performance of Shakespeare's *Richard III*. They returned the following year to present a new London success, Congreve's *The Constant Couple, or A Trip to the Jubilee*. Later in the same year the theatre was bought by the company of Lewis Hallam, who made its debut in the colonies with *The Merchant of Venice,* "before a numerous and polite audience, with great Applause." Wealthy planters flocked to the playhouse, sending slaves ahead to secure their choice box seats, and Hallam took in as much as £300 an evening. Governor Dinwiddie attended one performance of *Othello* with great ceremony, accompanied by the Cherokee emperor—with whom Virginia was negotiating a treaty—his wife, and young son. The empress was frightened by the mock duel in the play and hastily ordered her attendants to avert bloodshed! In later years George Washington once visited the theatre on five successive nights, perhaps to admire the beautiful Sarah Hallam, a popular actress who, after her retirement from the stage returned to Williamsburg to live and for a while kept a dancing school. The Revolution brought a long recess to the drama in the city, and the Second Theatre disappeared sometime before 1782.

The Blue Bell—W. Reconstructed. On this lot, granted in 1703 to John Redwood, keeper of the Public Gaol and caretaker of the Capitol, a large house was built sometime prior to 1707 and operated as an ordinary. Purchased by Colonel Philip Ludwell the

following year, it was owned by him and his heirs till 1832, and rented to a variety of tenants. Thomas Bramer had a shop here in which he carried wares ranging from Delft china to molasses—an assortment typical of his trade and times. By 1768 the building had become known as The Blue Bell. Its most unusual feature, established by archaeological findings, is a basement kitchen instead of a separate building. A later shed-roof addition is represented at the rear. Privately occupied.

Dr. Robert Waller House and Office—E. Unrestored. Benjamin Waller owned a large tract of land in this area in 1749, and sold a portion of it to Benjamin Powell in 1763. It is probable that Powell built the house which appears at this location on the Frenchman's Map of about 1782. Powell was a carpenter who became a successful contractor; in 1770 he undertook to construct the buildings for Eastern State Hospital for the sum of £1070. His rise to prominence, which typified that of other able and ambitious craftsmen of the period, culminated in his appointment to serve with Peyton Randolph, George Wythe, Robert Carter Nicholas, and other men of similar standing on a committee to enforce the boycott of British trade under the Continental Association. Powell sold the property in 1782. After changing hands several times, it was purchased by the son of Benjamin Waller and by him deeded to his son, Dr. Robert Waller, in 1814. The small brick building probably served as the doctor's office. Both buildings are privately occupied.

INDEX